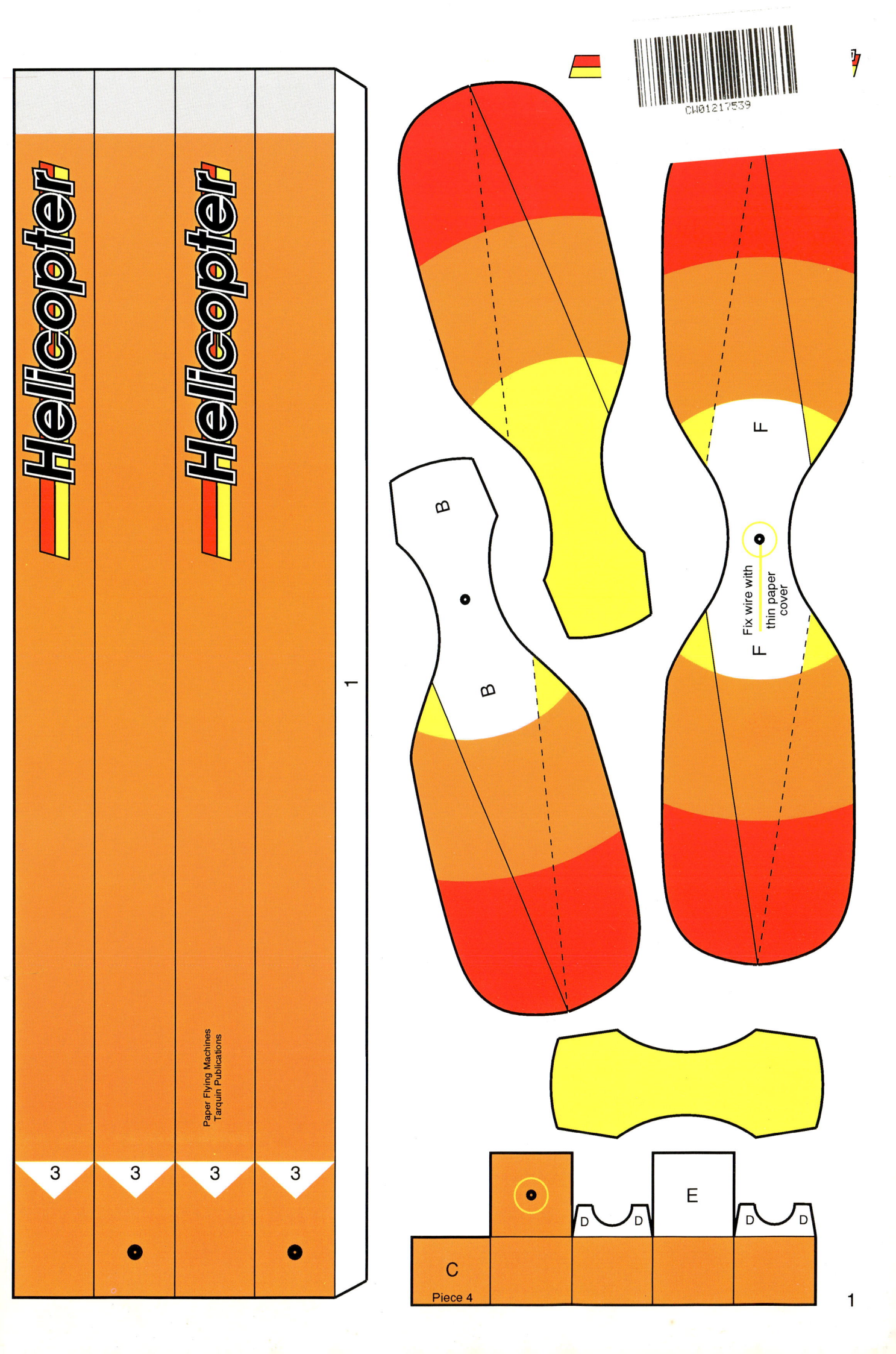

Helicopter

Helicopter

3 3 3 3

Paper Flying Machines
Tarquin Publications

1

B B

F
Fix wire with
thin paper
F cover

C
Piece 4

D D E D D

1

B

Helicopter
Power Unit
piece 3

B

A

B

A

B

Helicopter
Fuselage piece 1

1

A

Helicopter
Power Unit
piece 1

A

Helicopter
Power Unit
piece 2

Helicopter
Power Unit
piece 6

G   G

E

C

2

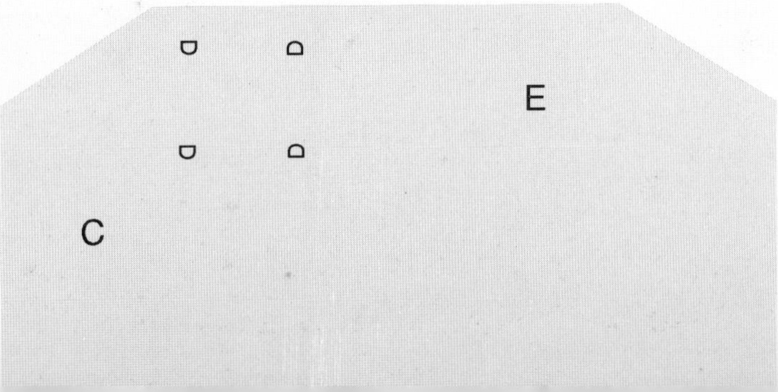

Deltawing

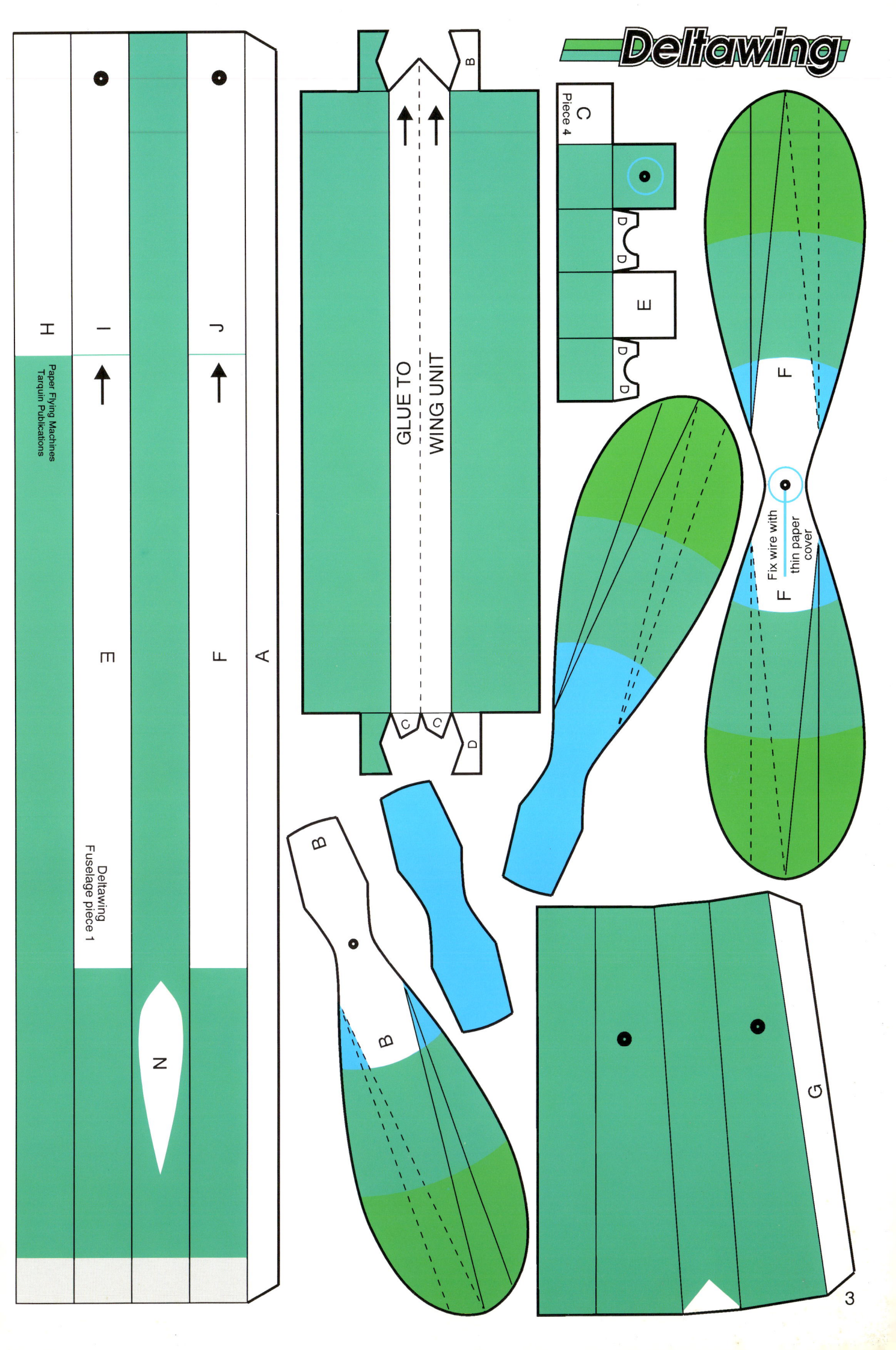

GLUE TO WING UNIT

C Piece 4

Fix wire with thin paper cover

Paper Flying Machines
Tarquin Publications

Deltawing
Fuselage piece 1

3

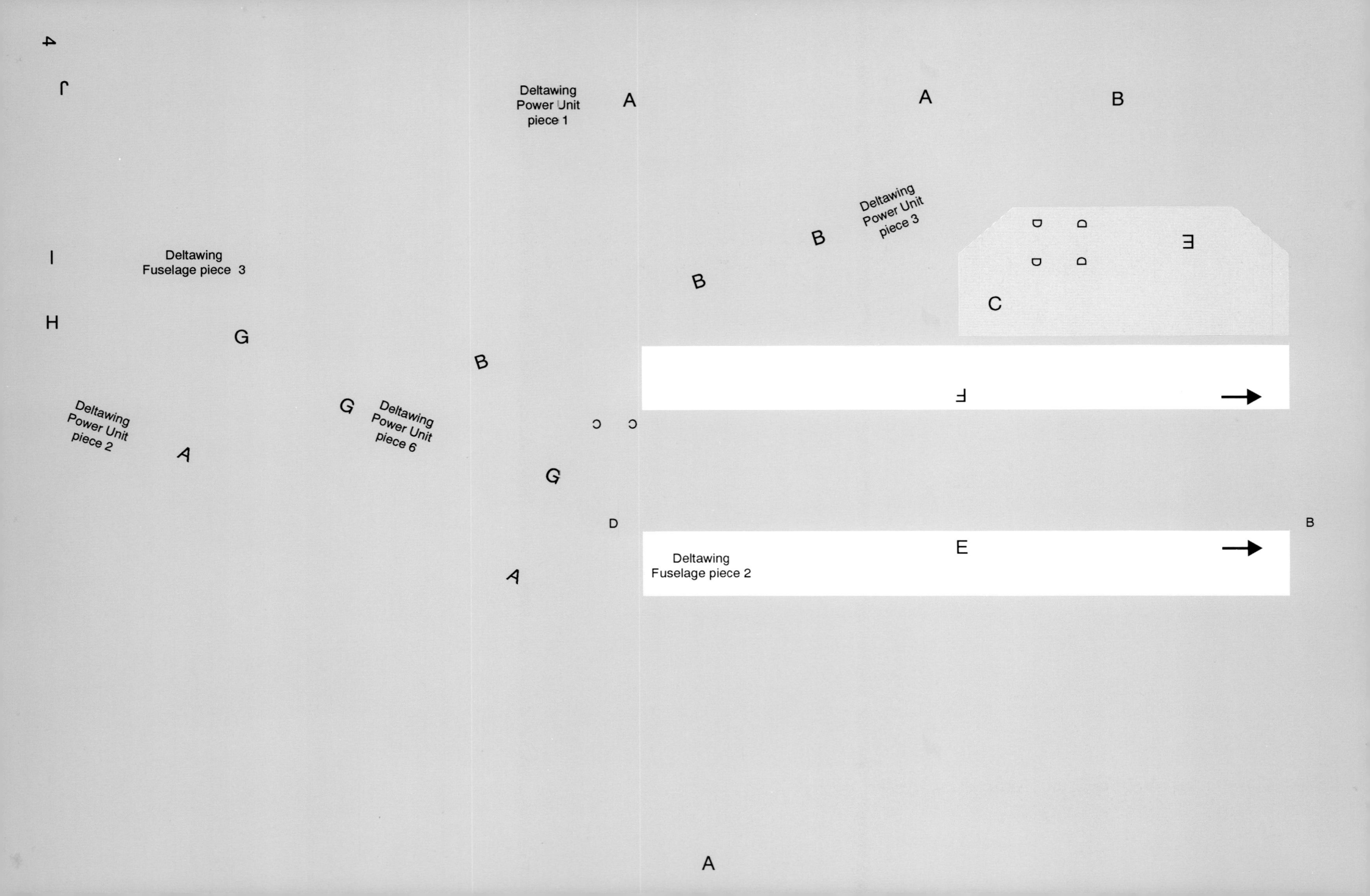

Deltawing Power Unit piece 1

Deltawing Power Unit piece 3

Deltawing Fuselage piece 2

Deltawing Power Unit piece 6

Deltawing Fuselage piece 3

Deltawing Power Unit piece 2

Deltawing

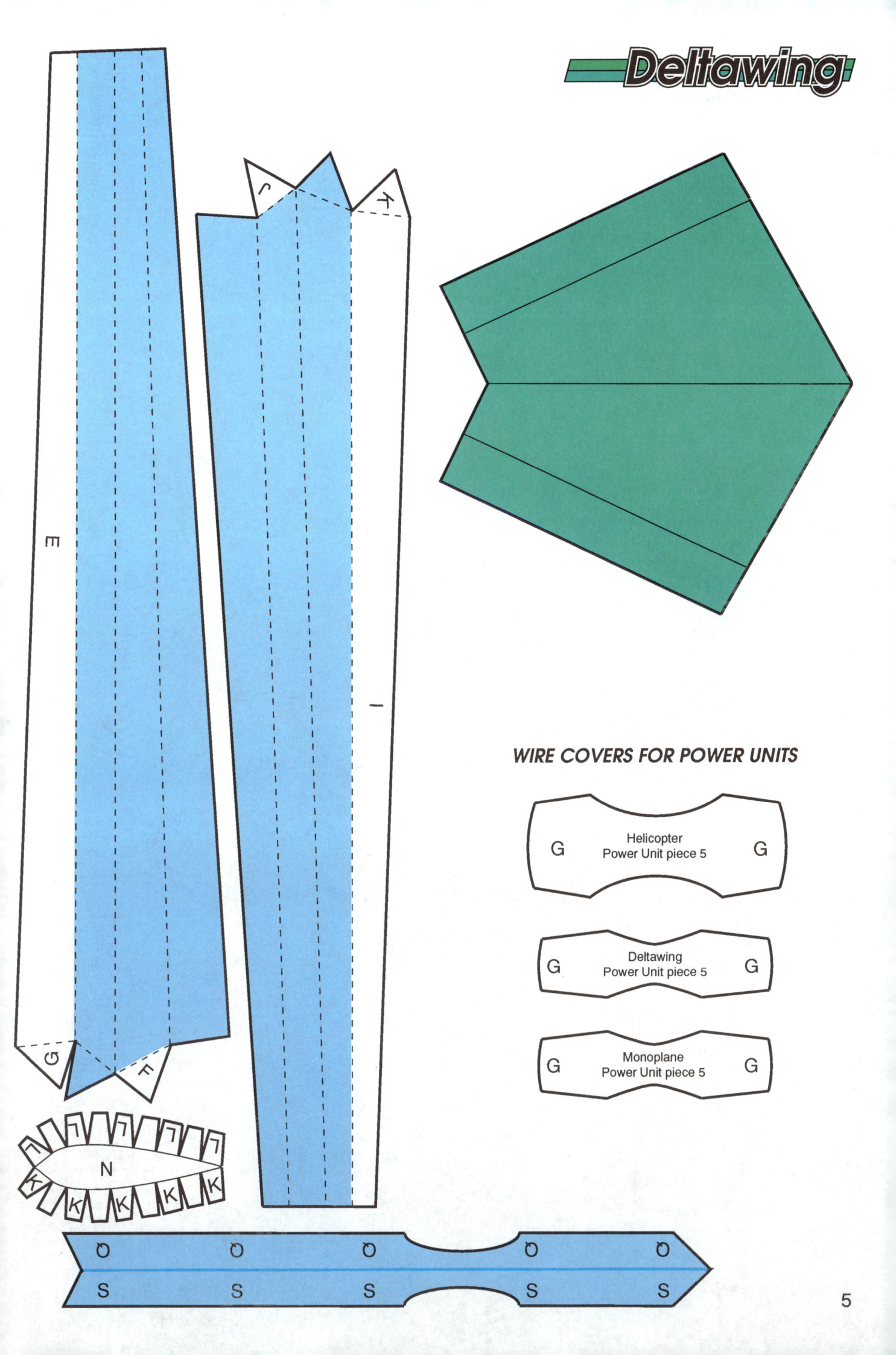

WIRE COVERS FOR POWER UNITS

G Helicopter Power Unit piece 5 G

G Deltawing Power Unit piece 5 G

G Monoplane Power Unit piece 5 G

5

Deltawing Wing Unit piece 5

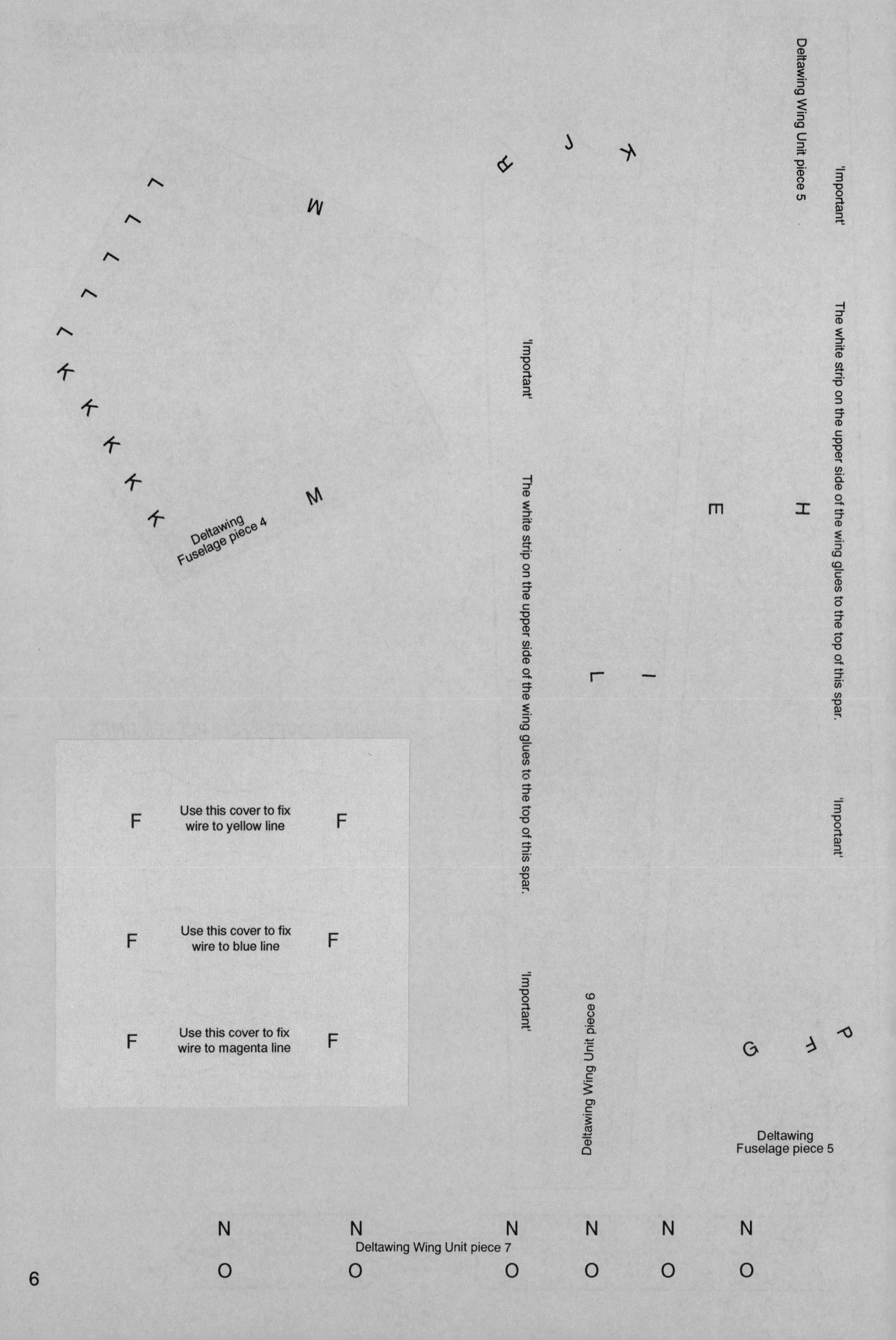

'Important'

The white strip on the upper side of the wing glues to the top of this spar.

J K
R

M

L L L L L
L
K
K
K
K
K
K
K
K

Deltawing Fuselage piece 4

M

'Important'

The white strip on the upper side of the wing glues to the top of this spar.

E H

L I

F	Use this cover to fix wire to yellow line	F
F	Use this cover to fix wire to blue line	F
F	Use this cover to fix wire to magenta line	F

'Important'

Deltawing Wing Unit piece 6

G F P

Deltawing Fuselage piece 5

N N N N N N
O O O O O

Deltawing Wing Unit piece 7

6

Deltawing

Deltawing Wing Unit piece 3

Deltawing Wing Unit piece 2

7

GLUE TO
WING UNIT

Deltawing

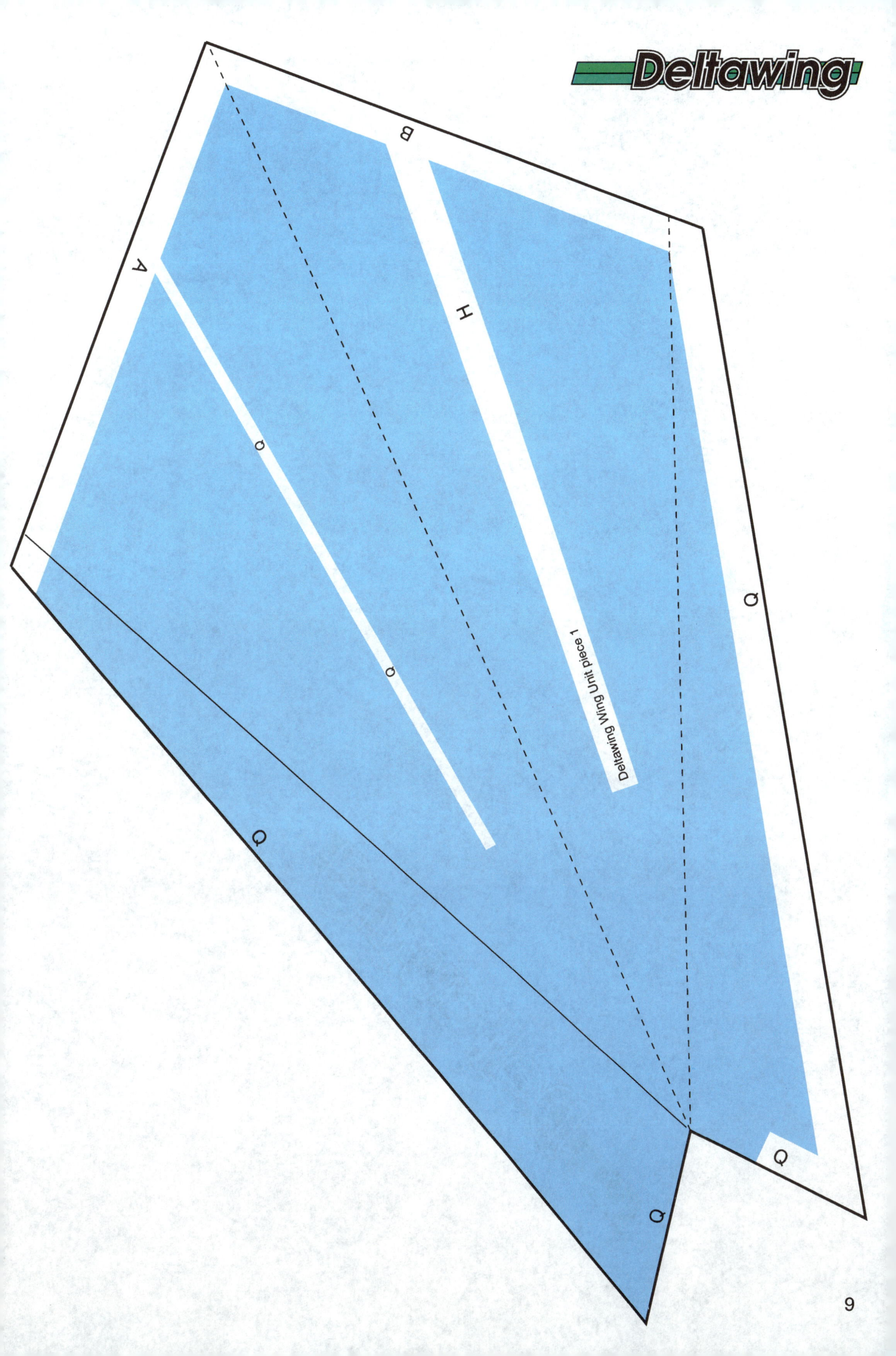

Deltawing Wing Unit piece 1

9

Deltawing

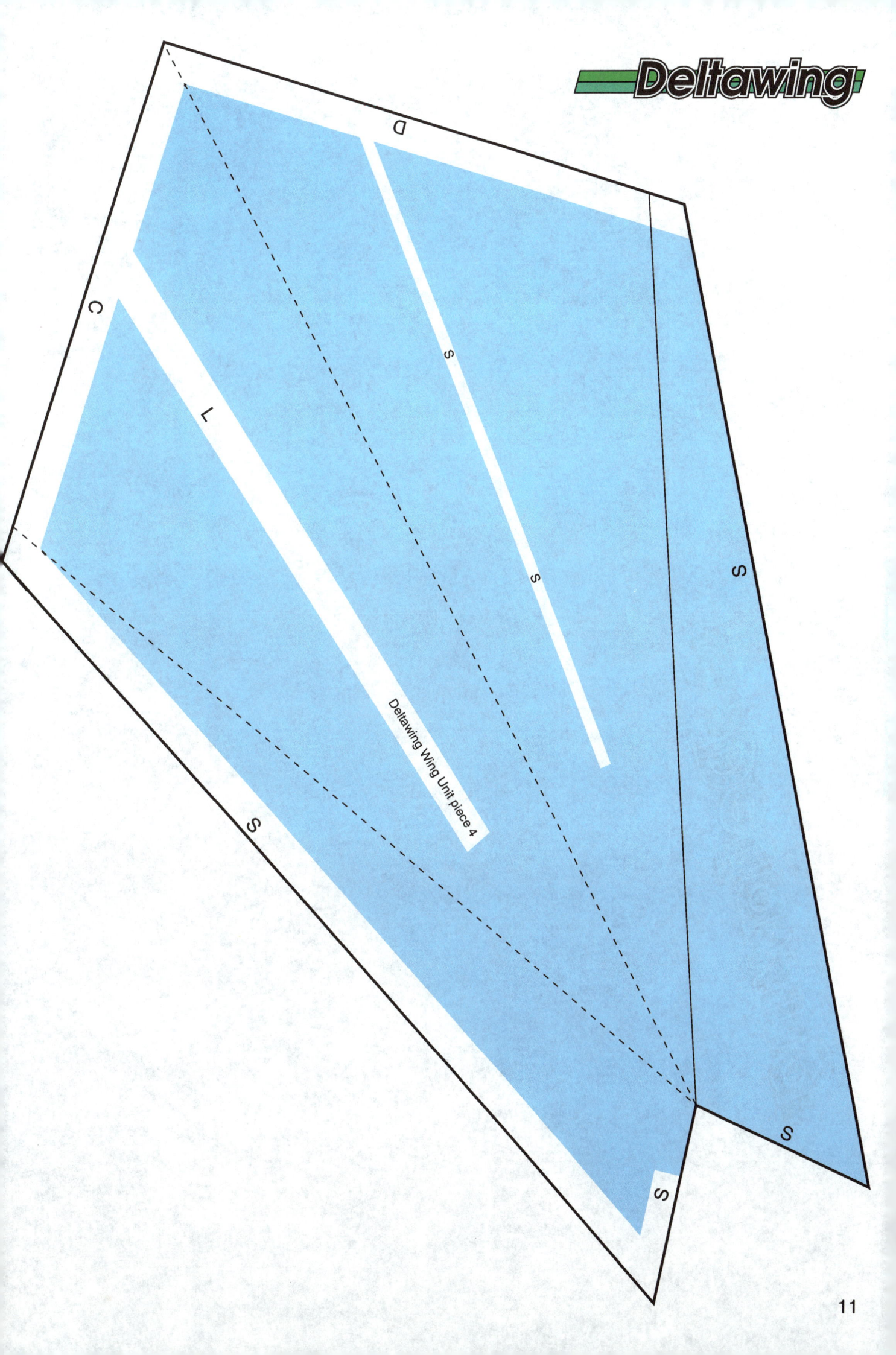

Deltawing

Deltawing Wing Unit piece 4

11

Deltawing

MINIBOOK SECTION A

The
FLIGHT MANUAL

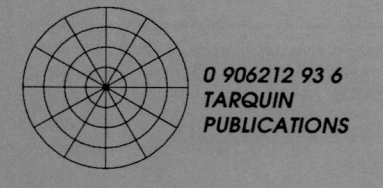

DRAG
LIFT
WEIGHT
THRUST

The principles & practice of flying real planes & models

John Andrews

0 906212 93 6
TARQUIN PUBLICATIONS

AN ART AND A SCIENCE

The aim of this minibook is to explain the underlying science which makes controlled flight possible and to use the three models to illustrate some of its most important and interesting principles. These paper models may seem to be very simple, but they still had to be designed using sound aeronautical ideas. Two of the models look rather like real planes but just because they look like them does not mean that they would automatically fly properly. They had to be carefully designed for the weight of paper to be used and then tested and modified many times before their performances became acceptable. The third model, the helicopter, does not look very much like a real helicopter, but none the less it does fly very well and offers genuine insights into the principles of hovering and climbing flight using rotors.

The design of aeroplanes is both an art and a science. This is true whether they are full size civil or military planes powered by jet engines or small paper models like the ones in this book powered by elastic. All of them have to obey the same laws of physics and aerodynamics if they are to fly successfully.

Real planes have to undergo long periods of test flights, modifications and trials with prototypes before they are ready for mass production. In theory, mass produced planes should all be identical but in practice they all differ from each other a little and need small adjustments to be made during the 'proving' flights before they can be delivered to the airline or the air force.

In a similar way these printed paper models are identical to the original design. However, in making them up, small differences will always occur. These small differences mean that each model has to be adjusted or 'trimmed' for flight. At the end of this minibook there is some good advice on how to trim your models and how to get them to fly well.

2

FLYING THE DELTAWING

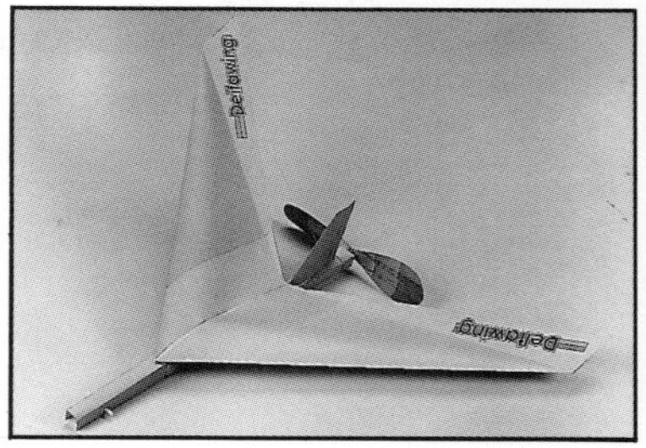

Deltawing designs are intrinsically more unstable and difficult to fly than designs like the monoplane and so we can expect to have to spend more time trimming and adjusting this model. It is more likely to stall at slow speeds and is particularly sensitive to small changes in the angles of the trailing edges of the wings. These trailing edges should be bent upwards, possibly as much as 20° at the tips.

There is no tailplane but the wing tips are far enough back to take over some of its function in providing stability against pitching.

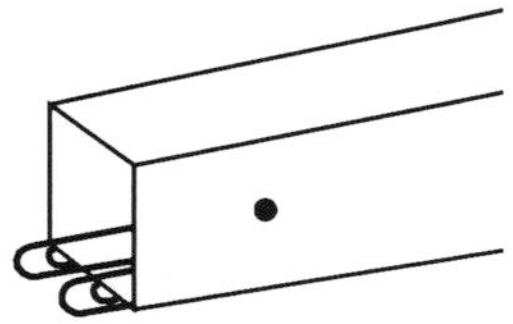

To glide or fly properly, the model needs a little more weight concentrated at the nose. This brings the centre of gravity of the model into the same vertical line as its centre of lift, about two thirds of the width of the wing from the front.

The most convenient way of adding the weight to the nose is to slide one or two paperclips over the lower edge. They also act as useful shock absorbers in the event of crash-landings.

When flying under power, the reaction from the propeller rotating in one direction causes a tendency for the Deltawing to roll in the opposite direction. This is a tendency in real planes as well although not as markedly as in helicopters. To counteract this, the trailing edge of the tail fin needs to be bent a little towards the left.

To undertake a test flight, hold the model with the propeller towards you and wind it about 70 turns in a clockwise direction. Then hold the fuselage horizontally at shoulder height, restraining the propeller with the other hand. Release the propeller, then gently push the model forwards on a level flight path, doing your best to prevent the propeller hitting the other hand! The model should fly straight and level. If it dives, bend up the trailing edges of the wings a little more. If it climbs steeply before stalling, the upward bend on the trailing edges may be too much and needs to be reduced. If the model veers to the right or left you will need to bend up one trailing edge a little more than the other. Small adjustments can have an important effect, so be patient and systematic. It will fly well.

When you are happy with short flights, gradually increase the number of turns until you reach a maximum of about 150.

Good flying!

If you have enjoyed this book then there may be other Tarquin books that will interest you, including 'Famous Balloon Mobiles' by Andy Hall. They are available from Bookshops, Toy Shops, Art/Craft Shops or, in case of difficulty, directly from Tarquin Publications, Stradbroke, Diss, Norfolk, IP21 5JP, England.

For an up-to-date catalogue of Tarquin books, please write to the publishers at the address above.

23

MINIBOOK SECTION B

SUPPORTED BY AIR

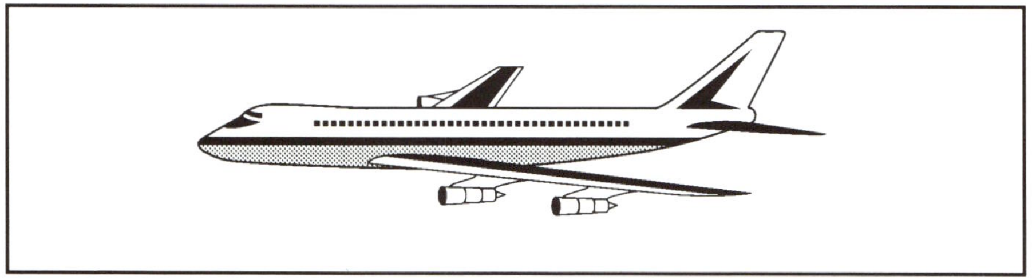

A visit to any major airport will soon dispel the notion that there is anything uncertain or haphazard about flying. At peak times a plane lands or takes off every minute or two. Indeed so universal and popular has flying become that it is estimated that, at certain times of day, more than one million human beings are in the air. If this sounds unbelievably many, then think of it as about 3000 fully loaded jumbo jets. If that also sounds a lot, then consider that just the single airport, London Heathrow, has over 500 aircraft movements a day.

This is all the more astonishing when we consider that the first manned powered flight took place in 1903 and lasted for only 12 seconds! The pilot had to lie flat in the middle of the wing, the plane could carry no passengers and the flight covered 37 metres only. However, once the principles of flight began to be understood, progress was very rapid indeed. Within six years Bleriot was able to fly across the English channel and within ten there were planes with four engines. By 1923, barely 20 years from that first flight, there were airlines carrying passengers on a regular basis.

A fully laden jumbo jet weighs 350 tonnes or more. Apart from carrying over 400 people, their luggage, food and water there is the weight of the enormous machine itself, including the fuel for the journey. It is a great surprise to many people that such a weight could possibly be supported by something as insubstantial and light as air. Some people find the whole idea so unlikely that they refuse ever to fly at all!

A CLASSIC DIAGRAM

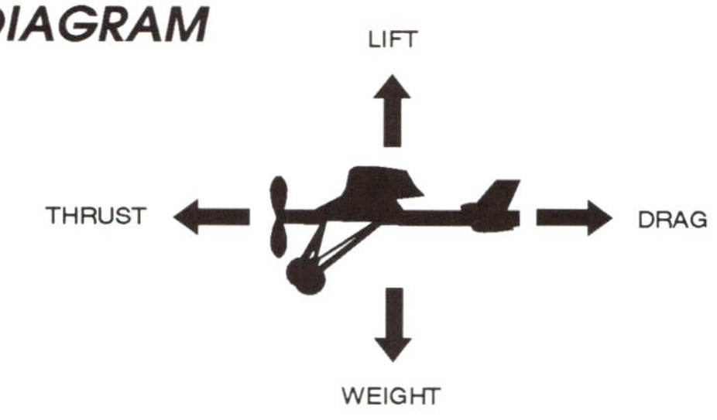

Most explanations of how aeroplanes fly start with a diagram like the one above. It shows four forces, two acting vertically and two acting horizontally. If both sets of forces are in balance then the plane will fly straight and level and at a constant speed.

Real planes seldom fly straight and level for long, so to gain a proper understanding of the physics of flight we need to understand about forces, velocities and accelerations. Then we shall be able to understand how planes can take off and land, dive and climb and how they can be designed to cope with the stresses of weather and the real world.

3

FLYING THE MONOPLANE

This model does look like a small plane of the past and indeed bears a strong resemblance to many which are in use today. It is a stable and robust design and needs little trimming to fly well.

The centre of lift is about one third of the width of the wing from the front and is just behind the position of the spar. To fly satisfactorily the centre of gravity needs to be in the same vertical line. It is likely that it will be but you can test it by balancing the model on a finger under each wing.

It is best to start the trials by checking its gliding capabilities. To do this, hold it by the fuselage just under the wing at about shoulder height and push it gently forwards and downwards. It should glide smoothly and land. If the plane dives too steeply, bend the trailing edge of the tailplane up a little. If the model climbs steeply and stalls, bend the trailing edge of the tailplane down a little.

You are now ready for the first powered test flight. Wind the motor up about 40 turns in a clockwise direction (with the propeller facing towards you). Hold the model at shoulder level with the other hand holding the propeller. Give the model a gentle push forwards and let go with both hands. It should fly and glide gently downwards in a straight line. If it veers to the left, bend the trailing edge of the tail fin to the right a little. Alternatively, if the plane veers to the right, bend the trailing edge of the tail fin to the left a little.

It is unlikely that the model will try to roll but notice how the wings wobble slightly in flight as the dihedral automatically corrects for level flight. However, if it does roll to the right, bend the trailing edge of the right wing tip down a little and the trailing edge of the left wing tip up a little. For a roll to the left, do the reverse.

When you are happy with short flights, try winding the motor 100 turns, then more, up to an absolute maximum of 150 turns. You can also experiment with adjusting the centre of gravity by adding a small piece of Blu-Tack to various places along the underside of the fuselage. Our experience is that this does not make very much difference but it is worth trying.

WILL IT TAKE OFF?

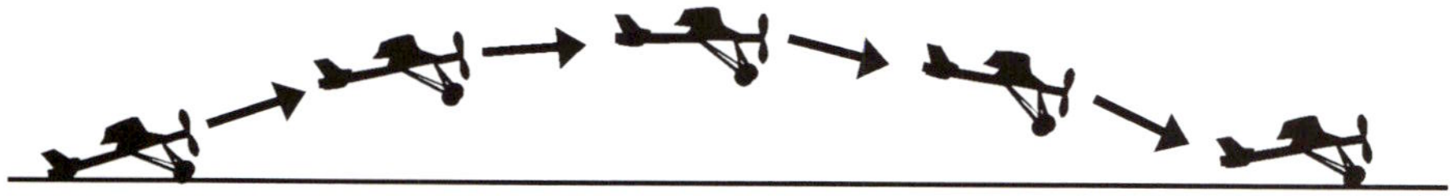

The answer is yes. You will need to find a smooth surface and still air. You will also need to check that the wheels turn freely. Wind the motor and, holding the propeller and the fuselage, set the plane down pointing in the direction in which you want it to take off. Release the propeller and the fuselage and watch it gather speed, take off, fly a certain distance and then land.

22

WEIGHT AND MASS

Our lives on earth are dominated by the action of the force of gravity. All objects, not forgetting our own bodies, are attracted towards the centre of the earth. In fact the word 'downwards' really means 'in the direction in which the force of gravity acts' and 'upwards' really means 'opposite to the direction in which the force of gravity acts'.

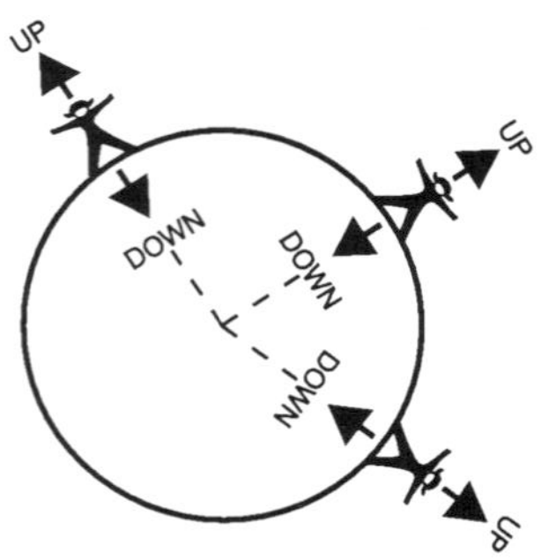

This diagram reminds us that these directions are different for people living in other parts of the world. It is important to keep in mind that the force of weight, whether of an aeroplane or a molecule of air always acts directly downwards no matter how quickly or in what direction it is moving.

In the course of ordinary speech, people do not usually distinguish between the mass and the weight of an object but in understanding the science of flight it is essential to appreciate the difference. Mass is a measure of the quantity of matter and it is measured in kilograms in the metric system or in pounds in the imperial system. Weight is the force of attraction due to gravity acting on that object and in the metric system it is measured in newtons or sometimes in kilograms weight. On the surface of the earth or close to it, in the region where aeroplanes fly, a mass of 1kg weighs 9.80665 newtons or 1 kg weight. In the imperial system a mass of 1 pound (lb) weighs 1 pound weight.

ADDING FORCES - CG

Every molecule of an aeroplane has mass and therefore has a force of weight acting vertically downwards. Of course, even the largest plane is very small compared to the size of the earth and so we can ignore the curvature and say that these forces are parallel. From the scientific point of view an aeroplane can be regarded as a 'rigid body' and these parallel forces can be added together to give a single 'resultant' force acting at a single point.

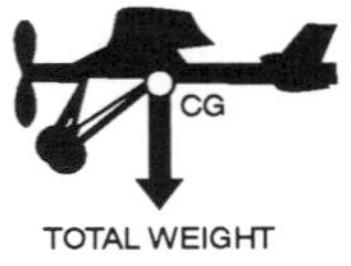

This single resultant force equal to the total weight of the plane replaces all the individual parallel forces of weight acting on every separate particle. The special point is known as the 'centre of gravity' or CG.

The CG of the model planes can be found by balancing them on two fingers. For the Monoplane and the Deltawing it lies about one third of the way along the body. For the Helicopter it lies about half way between the rotors.

The CG does not change its position within an aeroplane as it flies but exactly where it is situated is of the greatest importance in determining the flying performance of a model you have made is to change the position of the CG by adding extra weight in the form of paperclips or Blu-Tack to the nose or to the tail.

4

AUTOGIROS

The difference between an autogiro and a helicopter is that the blades of an autogiro are not driven directly by an engine except for a few moments before it takes off. Power for forward flight is provided by a conventional propeller. As the machine starts to move forwards, the rotors are disconnected from the engine and tilt backwards. The blades are then blown round by the relative airflow (autorotation). It is this that generates the lift.

Autogiros are usually very small, holding just one person. The advantage of this kind of machine is that it can fly very slowly and is highly manoeverable. It cannot, however, hover or make a vertical landing.

FLYING THE HELICOPTER

This model does not look very much like a conventional helicopter, but it uses the principles of helicopter flight to fly most satisfactorily. It will hit the ceiling of even a very high room. In a two-story house try releasing it in the stairwell. Outside, keep well away from buildings and roofs.

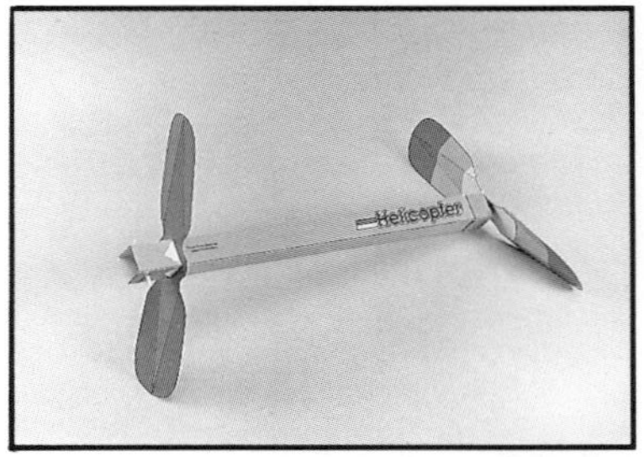

Probably, as it flies, you will tend to concentrate on the whirring rotors. However, do observe that the whole body spins in the opposite direction to the movement of the top rotors - exactly what a full-size helicopter would do if it had no tail rotor.

You might also like to experiment by winding the propeller in the opposite direction and then set it off with the moving rotors at the bottom. It will fly just about as well.

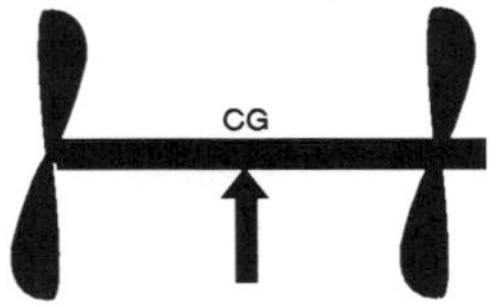

To fly the helicopter, hold it with the top rotors towards you and wind it up with about 100 turns in a clockwise direction. Hold it in a vertical position with the body in one hand and the top rotor in the other. Release the top rotor, let it spin a little and then release the body. The helicopter should fly straight upwards in a most satisfactory fashion.

The centre of gravity of the model is about half way between the rotors and it can be found by balancing the completed model on a finger. Both rotors provide lift and so the centre of lift must be in a similar position. However, this is not very critical as it is a very tolerant design. Because of the rapidly rotating parts it has some of the stability of a gyroscope. If you are particularly interested in this aspect of the design, make another model for yourself but leave the fixed rotor unglued to the body. You can then slide it up and down the body and see what happens when the centres of lift and gravity are in different positions. Try flying it both ways up.

The strength of pull given by the rotors depends on the angle at which the blades are set. For best results they need to be at about 45° to the horizontal at the tips. Because the rotors are contra-rotating the blades on the upper rotor should be twisted in the opposite direction to those of the lower. If you make a mistake and twist them both the same way you will find that the model will still rotate energetically but will sink to the floor and not rise into the air. One rotor is giving momentum to air molecules in one direction, the other in the opposite direction. The effects cancel out and there is no lift.

21

MINIBOOK SECTION C

VELOCITY AND ACCELERATION

The word velocity is used to describe the speed of an object in a given direction. We often talk about the speed of an aeroplane or a car, but it is more usual in scientific work to use the term 'velocity'. Because velocity includes the idea of direction, it is possible for an object to change velocity without changing speed. For example, when a car turns a corner without speeding up or slowing down, it is moving in a different direction so its velocity has changed. 'Acceleration' is the rate of change of velocity.

BALANCED AND UNBALANCED FORCES

Until the time of the scientist, Isaac Newton (1642-1727), most people thought that it required a force to make things move. Newton stated clearly in his first law that a force was required to make things change speed or direction. He realised that in the absence of a force, objects would continue to move in a straight line at a constant speed for ever. Remember that a stationary object can be thought of as moving at a constant speed of zero!

In understanding the science of flight we are mostly concerned with pairs of forces which act in opposite directions. These forces may either be balanced, in which case there is no resultant and no acceleration or they may be unbalanced, in which case there is an acceleration in the direction of the larger force.

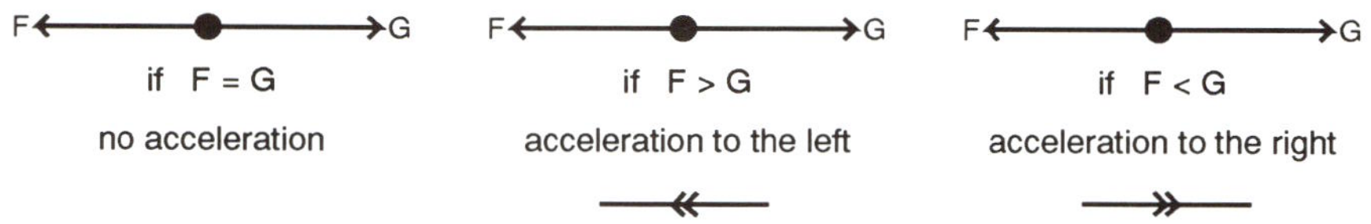

F→ ● →G   F→ ● →G   F→ ● →G

if F = G   if F > G   if F < G

no acceleration   acceleration to the left   acceleration to the right

Balanced forces mean that an object moves at a constant velocity
(which might be zero)

Unbalanced forces cause an object to change velocity
(which might mean that it starts to move or that it stops)

RESULTANTS AND COMPONENTS

All the forces acting at a point can be replaced by a single force, called the resultant. It is important to realise that the object will move in exactly the same way under the influence of this resultant force as it would under the influence of the original forces.

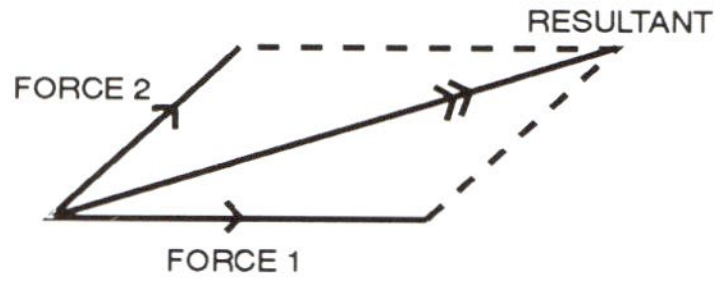

In a similar way a force can be replaced by two forces at right angles. This is known as 'resolving a force into components'. Since weight always acts vertically, it is usual to resolve the forces involved with flying into their horizontal and vertical components.

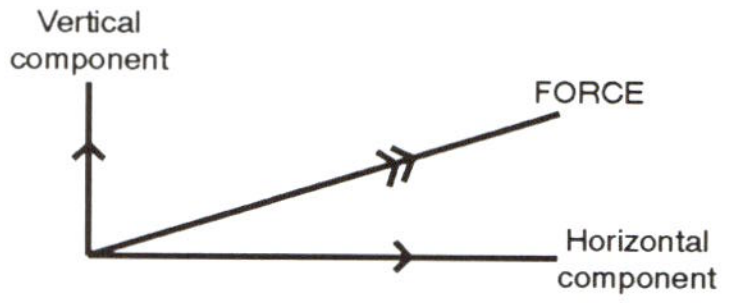

An aeroplane moves horizontally under the influence of its horizontal component and vertically under the influence of its vertical component.

LIFT FROM ROTORS

A rotor has an aerofoil section and is essentially a wing which rotates. As it rotates, air passes over its surface and generates lift in a similar way to any other kind of wing. The great advantage that a helicopter has over a fixed wing aircraft is that the machine itself does not have to move forwards in order to develop the lift. It can hover and has the ability to land or take off vertically. The word 'helicopter' really means 'spiral wing' because it screws itself through the air. The rotor tips trace out a spiral as the helicopter climbs or descends. To set against its considerable advantages, there are some serious disadvantages.

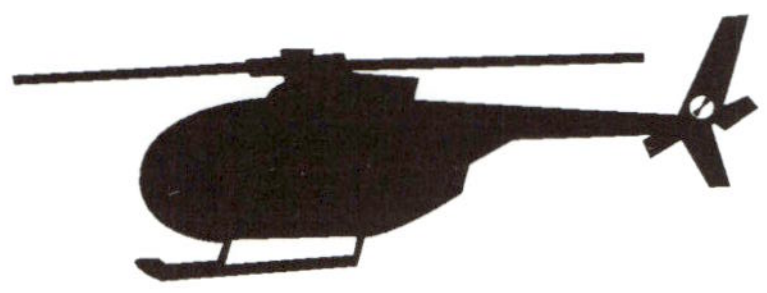

The first helicopter design was suggested by Leonardo da Vinci (1452-1519) but there were no engines available then which could drive it. There were other suggestions and designs in the succeeding centuries but when engines did become available, the engineering problems of control were also found to be formidable. It was 1942 before a reliable helicopter which could be mass produced was developed.

One problem which had to be overcome was that the reaction of the engine creates a turning moment on the fuselage in the opposite direction to the way that the rotor is turning. If a helicopter only had a single rotor, the fuselage would spin faster and faster. This disastrous possibility is avoided by having a smaller sideways-acting rotor in the tail. This tail rotor provides an equal and opposite turning moment which although small is absolutely essential. Many accidents with helicopters occur because the tail rotor becomes damaged. The pilot is then helpless as his cabin spins ever faster and uncontrollably. Some helicopters have twin lifting rotors turning in opposite directions in order to cancel out this torque. Such designs do not need a tail rotor, but it is a suitable solution only for very large machines.

A further problem which had to be solved was that whenever the helicopter begins to move horizontally, air flows over the machine as a whole. The air passes over the rotor blade more quickly when it is advancing than when it is retreating, inevitably generating uneven lift and the risk of rolling. The solution to this problem is a surprising one. The blades are hinged and allowed to flap! As they rotate they flap upwards when the lift is greater and downwards when it is less. This changing aspect alters the angle of attack and therefore helps to even out the lift. Even so, helicopters cannot fly as quickly as fixed wing planes.

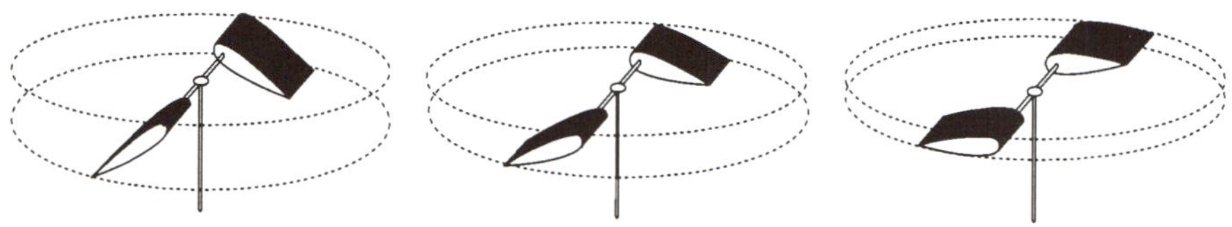

Climbing   Hovering   Descending

The vertical motion of a helicopter is controlled by the 'collective pitch stick' which alters the angle of attack of the rotor blades, thus increasing or reducing the amount of lift which is generated. To move forwards, backwards or sideways the pilot has another control called the 'cyclic control stick' with which he can tilt the whole rotor assembly. This tilt means that the force of lift has a horizontal component which then propels the helicopter in the direction in which the pilot wishes to fly.

ACTION AND REACTION

Sometimes it is not easy to recognise forces and is only too easy to forget them. This is particularly true of passive or 'reactive' forces. A simple example of someone standing on a solid floor or on thin ice is a useful illustration of whether forces are balanced or unbalanced.

When someone stands on the floor or other solid ground, the weight still acts vertically downwards. Since he does not fall or begin to move, there must be another force acting upwards to balance the weight. Such forces are known as 'reactions'. We need to be aware that the floor is pushing upwards on our feet with a force exactly equal to our weight.

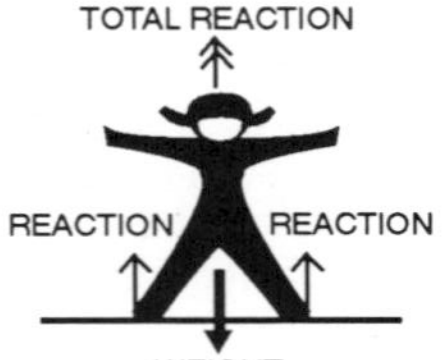

What happens when we stand on thin ice, is that the surface is not sufficiently strong to provide a large enough reaction to bear our weight. The forces are then unbalanced and the downwards force is greater than the upwards force. We therefore move in the direction of the greater force. In common speech we say that 'we fall through the ice'.

FORCES UP AND FORCES DOWN

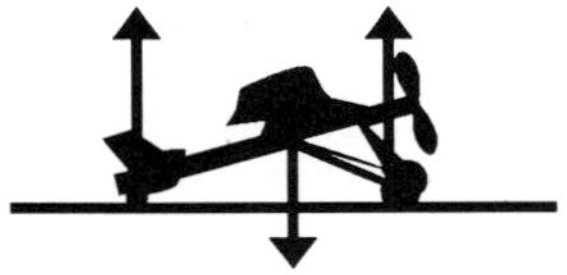

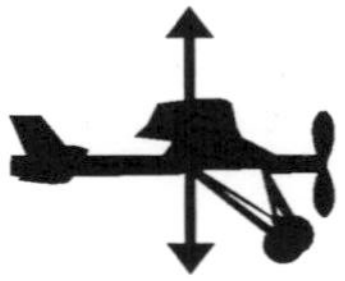

When a plane is on the ground its weight is balanced by an upward acting reaction from the ground acting through its wheels.

When the plane is in the air and flying horizontally, it is not accelerating upwards or downwards. There must therefore be an upwards acting force provided by the air. Forces of this kind are called 'lift'. There are three main sources of lift which are used to make manned flight possible.

THREE KINDS OF LIFT

It is possible to get lift from …

… a balloon filled with a gas that is lighter than air….

… wings as long as the plane is moving forwards …

… rotors as long as they are turning.

The lift from balloons is called 'static lift' as it does not require power or an engine to maintain it. The other types are called 'dynamic lift' and depend on motion in some way. To be able to understand any kind of lift, we must first have a good understanding of the nature of air.

6

DESIGNING FOR STRENGTH AND LIGHTNESS

Aircraft fly in order to take passengers and freight from one place to another and so it is the useful weight or payload which matters. This means that the weight of the structure itself must be kept as low as possible. However the aircraft designers must be careful to make sure that it has sufficient strength to meet the loads which will be placed upon it.

Although our models do not take passengers or freight they face exactly the same problems. Paper is not the strongest of materials and the elastic motor has only modest power, so they also had to be designed to have the maximum strength for the least possible weight. You will have noticed that the wings are made from much lighter paper than that of the fuselage and the power units. This was essential. Had the planes weighed just a few grammes more, there would not have been enough power stored in the elastic to generate sufficient lift. The ratio between the power available and the total weight is known as the 'power to weight' ratio. Within reason, the higher this ratio the better a plane will fly.

One way of economising on weight while maintaining strength is to use triangles wherever possible. You will see many triangles included in the design of the models.

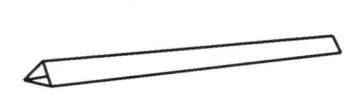

The wing spars are folded to give a tube with a triangular cross-section.

The Monoplane has triangular struts which form triangles to hold the wings in position.

The Deltawing wings are already triangles and therefore need no further support.

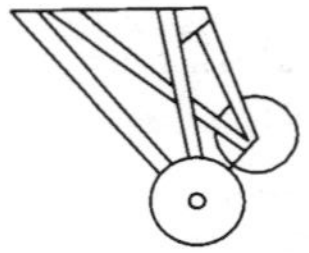

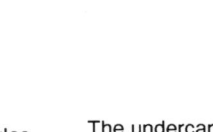

The undercarriage is a network of triangular struts arranged into triangular patterns.

ABSORBING SHOCK

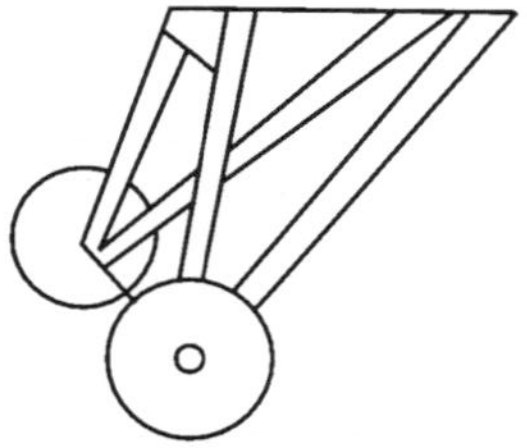

All aircraft components need strength, but they also need resilience. You will notice that the struts which form the undercarriage are not glued together where the axle passes through. This gives a certain amount of springiness. It is possible that you will be unlucky and a crash may cause the spars to break and have to be repaired. However, in general people are surprised that the Monoplane can crash-land so often and yet not damage itself. This is due, in great part, to the shock-absorbing aspects of the design.

When many people fly in a commercial aircraft for the first time they look out of the window and are horrified to see the wings flexing up and down. How, they think, could such a huge airliner have wings which seem not to be strong enough to hold the plane up properly? However, this flexibility is an essential part of their strength. Just like grass or trees bending before the wind, if they did not give a little under the buffeting of the air, they would soon break off.

19

MINIBOOK SECTION D

WHAT IS AIR?

Air is a mixture of the molecules of nitrogen, oxygen, carbon dioxide, water vapour and small quantities of rare gases like neon, xenon, krypton, etc. Its exact composition is not important in understanding flying, but the fact that air consists of particles is most significant.

Molecules are never still. At room temperature they move with an average velocity of about 450 metres/sec. They bounce off each other and any surface which they meet. Every time they hit anything they give it a small push and bounce off in a different direction. Anyone who has ever played billiards, snooker or pool has a good idea how balls bounce off each other and the cushions. Of course, molecules are not really like billiard balls at all, but it does give us a convenient mental picture of them to think of them in that way. The vital point to realise is that the molecules are very small indeed and that in any significant quantity of air there are billions or trillions of them. All are moving about at the same time and bouncing off each other millions of times every second in random directions. Because there are so many molecules and they are each so small, it is not possible for us to detect them individually. We can, however, detect the effect of the millions of impacts which they make on any surface. The total effect is the force we call 'air pressure'. Air pressure acts in all directions and at sea-level it is just under 15 lbs weight/sq.inch or 1.033 bars (a bar is 1 kg weight/square centimetre or 98,066.5 newtons per square metre). Because of the random motion, about the same number of molecules strike a surface no matter in which direction it faces.

What we call 'still air' is far from being still. The expression just means that the motion of molecules in one direction is, on average, equal to the movement of those in the opposite direction. What we call a wind, a draught or an airflow is the movement of billions of air molecules from one place to another. What makes air move is difference of pressure. It moves from an area of high pressure (where the molecules on average are denser) to one of a lower pressure (where they are less dense). However, in even the strongest wind, at any instant large numbers of molecules are going the opposite way.

WHAT IS THE AIR PRESSURE?

Imagine a column of air with a rectangular cross-section reaching from the surface of the earth out into space. The air pressure at any point in that column must support the weight of all the molecules above it. How otherwise could they remain there? The impacts of the molecules at sea-level support the whole column of air. Higher in the atmosphere there are fewer molecules above that level and so the pressure needed to support them is less. At 100,000 ft (30 km) the air pressure and the density of molecules are each approximately one hundredth of that at sea-level.

The area of this rectangle is 20 sq cm. If we imagine a column of air standing on it vertically and reaching right to the edge of the atmosphere some 500 km overhead, we know that the total weight of that column must be 20 x 1.033 kg = 20.66 kg, because the air pressure at sea-level is 1.033 bars. The weight of air above an area of 1 sq metre is just over 10 tonnes.

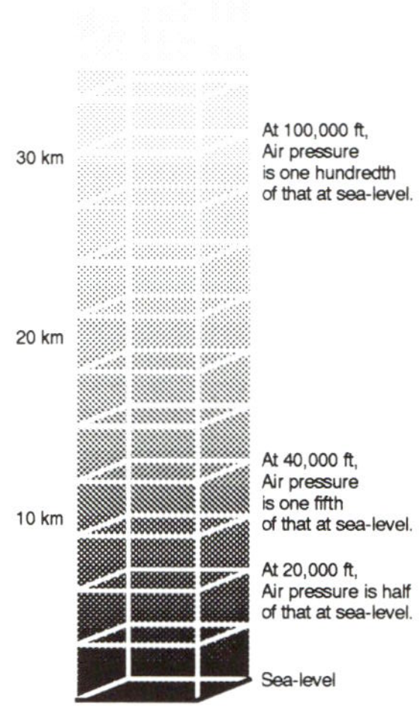

At 100,000 ft, Air pressure is one hundredth of that at sea-level.
At 40,000 ft, Air pressure is one fifth of that at sea-level.
At 20,000 ft, Air pressure is half of that at sea-level.
Sea-level

THE PARTS OF A JUMBO JET

flight deck, fuselage, fuel tanks inside wings, engines, undercarriage, ailerons, radio aerial, fin, tailplane, rudder, elevators

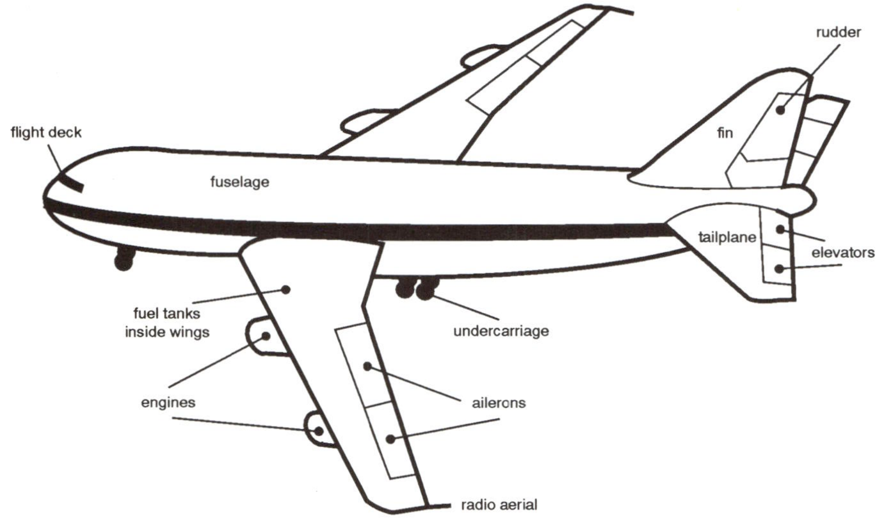

WING LOADING

Type	Max. weight	Wing area	Loading
Tornado	20,400 kg	26.6 m²	767 kg/m²
Boeing 747	377,800 kg	510.9 m²	740 kg/m²
Concorde	185,000 kg	358.2 m²	516 kg/m²
Radio controlled glider	5 kg	1.5 m²	3.3 kg/m²
Monoplane (inc. tail area)	0.025 kg	0.0480 m²	0.52 kg/m²
Deltawing	0.024 kg	0.0445 m²	0.54 kg/m²

This table shows the ratio of the weight of the aircraft to the wing area of several well-known planes plus our paper models. It is remarkable just how different they are. Because the lift obtainable from any wing goes up as the square of the speed, each square metre of wing can support vastly different loads at different speeds. These figures show the maximum loading at take-off. An aeroplane which was overloaded would need a higher speed along the runway before it could take off and perhaps the runway would not be long enough. For this reason the total weight on a commercial flight is rigorously monitored before flight clearance is given.

In a commercial jet the engines take up about 10% of the take-off weight and the fuel for a long flight up to 35% more, leaving only 55% for the remainder of the structure and the payload. A jumbo may start its flight with as much as 140 tonnes of fuel aboard. In the Monoplane and Deltawing models the power unit accounts for between 25% and 30% of the total weight and in the Helicopter almost 50%. Fortunately they do not require an additional allowance for fuel!

HOW MUCH DOES AIR WEIGH?

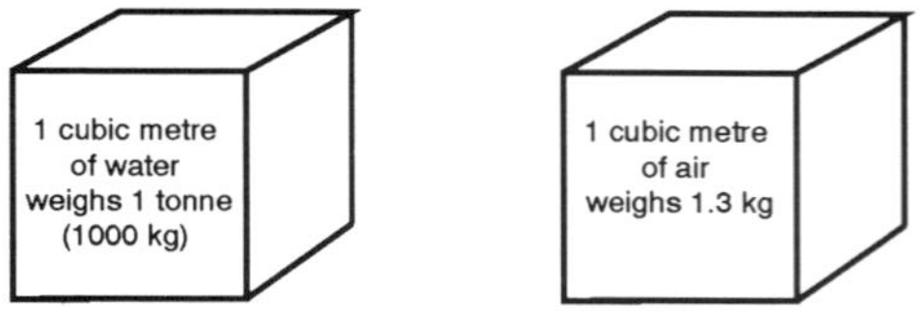

A human being is on average just a little less dense than water and when we immerse ourselves in it we float, but only just. People who are learning to swim fear that they will sink and drown, but once they become confident, they learn to relax and find that they are able to float with their noses and mouths just above the water surface. However, common sense tells us that no matter how much we relax, we cannot fly without mechanical assistance! To understand why this is, we need to think about 'upthrust', the upwards acting forces in fluids such as water and air.

A THOUGHT EXPERIMENT

Scientists like to do practical experiments but they also like to explain and prove things purely by thinking, wherever possible. This is a very good example of a 'thought experiment' because it clearly proves that any object immersed in a liquid or gas must experience an upthrust.

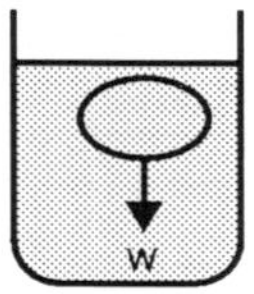

Let us first think about the upthrust in water in a container. Let us imagine enclosing a quantity of the water by an imaginary boundary surface and then think about it separately from the remainder. This 'piece' of water has some mass and must be attracted by the earth's gravity.

If there were no other forces acting on it besides its weight, this mass would sink to the bottom of the container. However we did not start by saying how big our 'piece of water' was or where it was situated. In other words any quantity of the water which we happened to think about would sink to the bottom. This is plainly nonsense. There must be an upwards acting force which balances its weight. Hence any quantity of water, whatever its shape or position, must experience a balancing force or 'upthrust' exactly equal to its weight. This upthrust is provided by the impacts and repulsions of the molecules in the surrounding water.

Now let us immerse an object in water. It will replace a certain quantity of the water, which we already know experiences an upthrust exactly equal to its weight. The molecules of water surrounding the object still repel and strike its surface in just the same way as they would repel and strike a 'piece' of water of exactly the same size and shape.

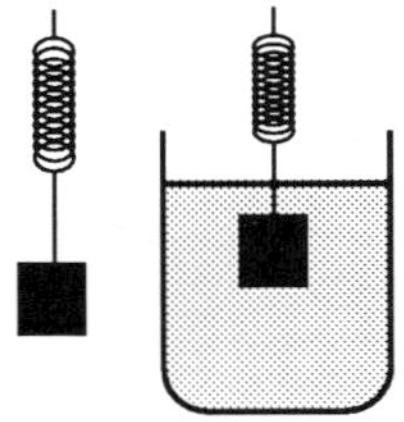

If you have a spring balance you can do a simple experiment and both see and measure the upthrust. Suspend an object from the balance and note its weight. Then lower it into some water and see how the apparent weight is reduced by the upthrust. Since the density of water is 1gm/cc and the upthrust is equal to the weight of water displaced you can calculate the volume of the object, no matter how complicated its shape. This law is known as 'Archimedes Law' and is named after the Ancient Greek scientist and philosopher.

1 cubic metre of water weighs 1 tonne (1000 kg)

1 cubic metre of air weighs 1.3 kg

HOW IS A GLIDER POWERED?

A glider has no engine and therefore cannot provide thrust or impart momentum to air molecules. How then can it fly?

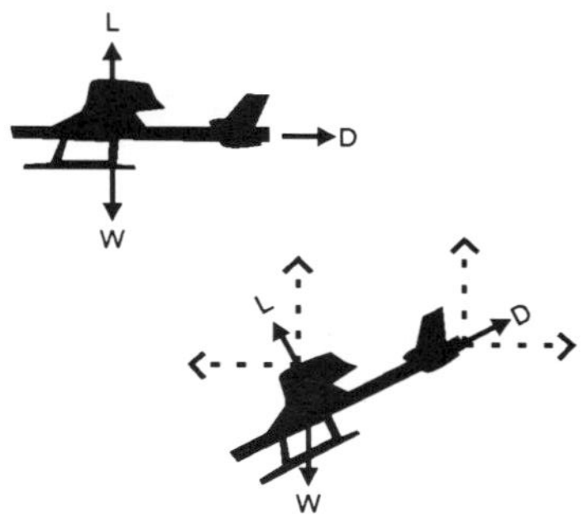

We have now used forces and force diagrams enough to see clearly that the upper diagram is nonsense. A glider can never fly straight and level. The forces do not balance.

However the lower and rather exaggerated diagram shows that when a glider dives, both the lift and drag are each resolved into two components: the vertical and the horizontal. It is the horizontal component of the lift which provides the thrust to take the plane forwards.

A glider is therefore propelled by its own weight. It is always flying downhill relative to the air!

The skill in designing a glider is to give it a very low sink rate. It can then travel as far as possible horizontally before it loses all its vertical height and has to land. Gliders are lifted into the air either by a towrope attached to a powered plane or from a ground based winch. The towrope gives the glider a forward speed and the lift from the wings then causes it to rise. From then on it is all downhill unless it can find places where the air itself is rising. These rising columns of air are called thermals. Although the glider still descends relative to the air it can rise relative to the ground.

THERMALS

Warmer air has a lower density than cold air and therefore rises. If the sun shines on to a certain surface, such as a road or an area of rock, the air above it warms up more quickly than nearby vegetated areas and may begin to rise. Glider pilots and those flying radio-controlled gliders become highly skilled at spotting thermals. Once such a rising column of air is found, a glider can circle within it and rise to considerable heights. By repeating this procedure whenever a thermal is encountered gliders are able to make long journeys across country.

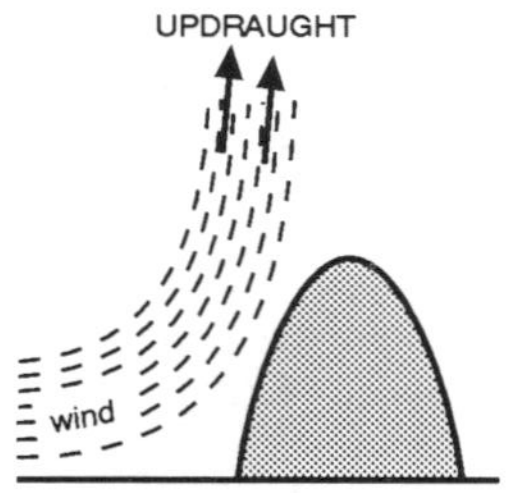

Another way of gaining height is to use the updraught from cliffs or from hills with steep sides. Glider clubs are often based on top of hills which are known to provide a reliable column of rising air. After a short tow the gliders can gain sufficient height by flying back and forth within this updraught to make a long and interesting flight possible.

Birds often use thermals and updraughts in order to soar or gain height. You may see gulls at the seaside riding the updraught from the cliffs. Birds like swifts, which even sleep on the wing, use thermals to gain height and then sleep as they slowly glide downwards.

With your elastic powered planes, you will get longer flights if you can find a thermal to lift them higher. Unfortunately, because of their light weight and sensitivity to wind, you cannot use an updraught from a cliff or a steep hill as do full-size or radio-controlled gliders. However, you can try to find thermals which develop over areas of concrete when the sun is shining.

MINIBOOK SECTION E

STATIC LIFT

The lift or upthrust on any object immersed in water experiences an upthrust equal to the weight of water displaced. Similarly the lift or upthrust on any object immersed in air experiences an upthrust equal to the weight of air displaced. A human weighing 80 kg will displace about 80.5 kg of water but only 0.1 kg of air. Thus we can float in water without any mechanical assistance, but need to make use of other forms of lift if we are to fly.

A balloon with a volume of one cubic metre displaces 1.3 kg of air and therefore experiences an upthrust or 'lift' equal to a weight of 1.3 kg. To float in air the total weight, *including the air or other gas inside*, must be less than 1.3 kg. The most efficient balloon would be one which contained a perfect vacuum as the contents would then weigh nothing at all. However it is impossible to make a one cubic metre vacuum container weighing less than 1.3 kg which is strong enough to withstand the pressure. To avoid the problem with the pressure we have to fill the balloon with a gas which is lighter than the surrounding air.

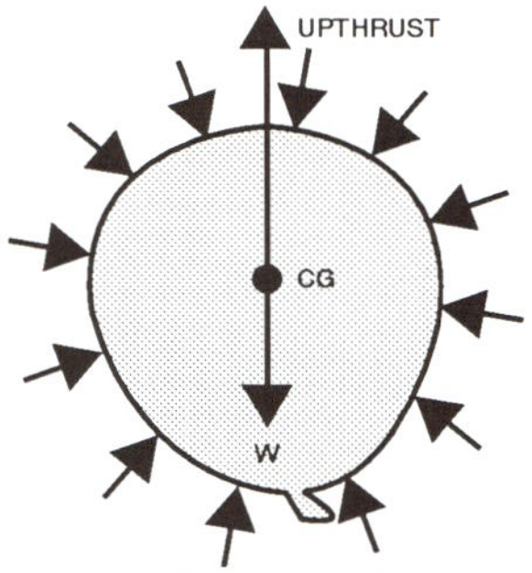

The upthrust is equal to the total weight of air displaced

The natural choices are helium or hydrogen. A cubic metre of hydrogen weighs 0.09 kg, so the fabric and structure of the balloon can be as much as 1.21 kg and it will still float in air. Helium is slightly less efficient (0.18 kg leaving 1.12 kg for the fabric of the balloon), but has the great advantage of being inert. Hydrogen is dangerously explosive and there were many accidents when it was used to fill balloons and airships.

HOT-AIR BALLOONS

The first manned flight in a hydrogen filled balloon was made on December 1st 1783, but the very first manned flight of all was made not in an aeroplane or a hydrogen balloon but in one filled with hot air. On the 21st November 1783 two Frenchmen, the Marquis d'Arlandes and François Pilatre de Rozier, made history by flying for five and a half miles in 25 minutes in a hot-air balloon designed and built by the Montgolfier brothers. This 'Montgolfière', as the French still call their hot-air balloons, made a colourful sight as it drifted across the skies of Paris from the Bois de Boulogne.

Nowadays hot-air ballooning is a popular sport and most of us have at some time seen a hot air balloon float overhead and have heard the roar of its gas jets.

We are now in a position of being able to understand why heating the air causes the balloon to rise. In hot air, the molecules move faster and so they each strike the inside of the balloon with more force. The pressure inside and outside remains the same because the balloon is open at the bottom but it requires fewer molecules inside to provide this pressure and so they weigh less. The lift generated by this difference is sufficiently great to support the balloon itself, the gas cylinders, burners and basket and also several passengers. By controlling the temperature of the air inside the balloon by igniting the burners in bursts, the height of the balloon can be quite well controlled and a reasonably gentle landing guaranteed.

CONTROLLING YAW

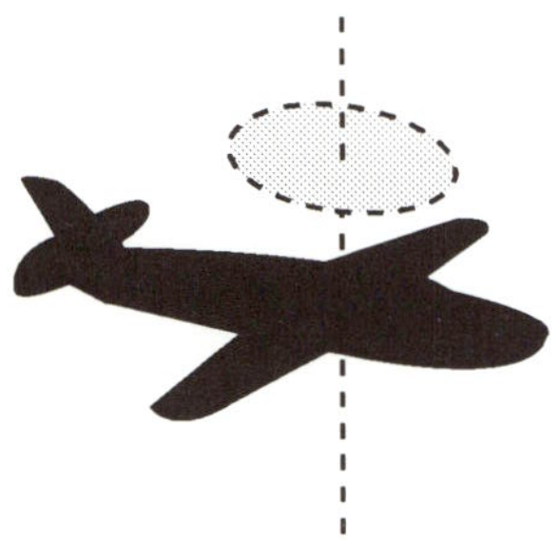

When a plane yaws, the nose moves around to a different heading from the direction of motion and air no longer flows evenly over the wings or along the fuselage. This changes both the amount and the direction of the forces of drag. A plane that begins to yaw can be very difficult to control.

The tail fin is the main method of controlling yaw automatically. Its cross-section is that of a symmetrical aerofoil and air passing over it in any direction but head on, generates a restorative force. The turning moment of this force is greater the further the fin is from the centre of gravity and therefore its stabilising effect is stronger. This effect is yet another reason why the Monoplane is more stable than the Deltawing.

Real planes have a moveable rudder at the rear of the fin. The pilot can use this to correct yaw developing, but contrary to popular opinion it is not used to turn corners. It is a common misconception that the rudder acts like the rudder on a boat when the plane has to change direction.

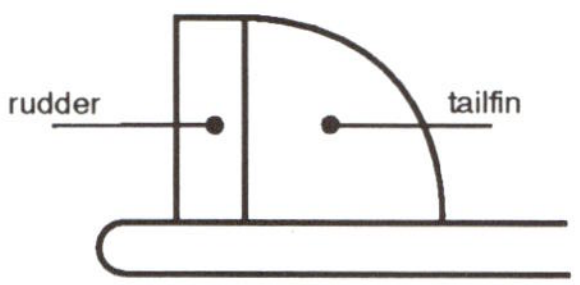

HOW TO MAKE A PROPER TURN

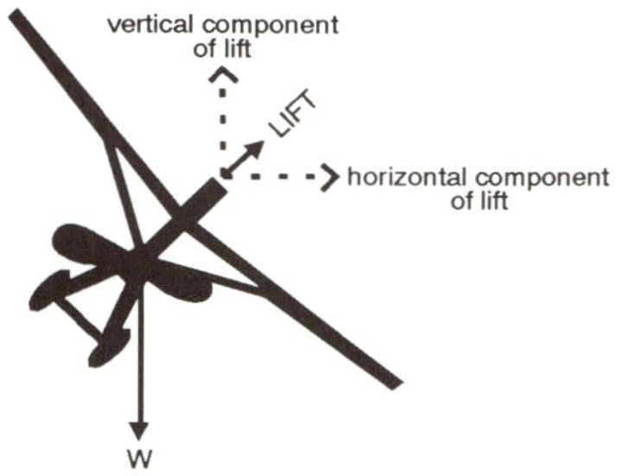

For an aircraft to execute a turn there has to be a horizontal force which is sufficiently great and the rudder is not large enough to provide it. The technique is to roll the plane so that the horizontal component of lift provides the horizontal force required. Rolling also reduces its vertical component and so the lift has to be increased to compensate. Unless the vertical component balances the weight, the plane will begin to descend. The lift must therefore be increased by using the ailerons to alter the effective angle of attack. To overcome the extra drag some extra thrust is also needed. This rather complicated manoeuvre requires some rudder control but if used to excess, a skidding turn is achieved and this might lead to a dangerous sideslip.

The exact combination of roll, yaw and throttle needed to make a turn is dependant on the characteristics of the individual aircraft, but many need no rudder movements at all. Unlike the steering wheel of a car which is kept rotated until the turn is complete, the joystick is returned to a neutral position once the desired amount of cornering is achieved. Otherwise, the turning movement would continue to tighten. When the required turn is complete, the joystick is then moved in the opposite direction to bring the plane on to its new heading.

DYNAMIC LIFT FROM WINGS

The weight of air displaced by an aeroplane is far less than its actual weight and so the static upthrust is not important in enabling a plane to remain in the air. The lift is generated by the shape of the wings as they move forwards. They have what is called an aerofoil section.

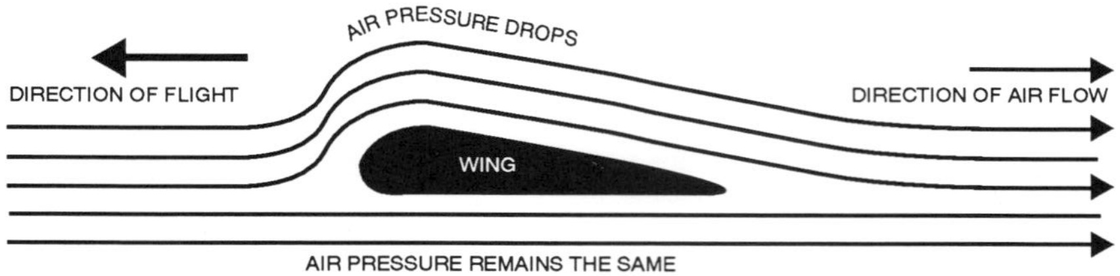

DIRECTION OF FLIGHT

AIR PRESSURE DROPS

WING

AIR PRESSURE REMAINS THE SAME

DIRECTION OF AIR FLOW

An aerofoil wing section divides the airflow into two streams which behave differently. There is a law of aerodynamics, called Bernouilli's theorem which connects the square of the speed of an airflow and its pressure. It states that as the speed of flow increases, the air pressure decreases. Those molecules of air passing above the wing flow in a curve and increase their average speed, thus reducing the pressure there. Those passing under the wing do not change speed and the pressure remains unchanged. This difference in pressure between the upper and lower surfaces of the wing generates an upwards force which is called the 'lift'. It is a dynamic force because it only exists when the plane is in motion. Lift acts at right angles to the wing surface at all points on it but can be summed into a single resultant force from a single point. This point is known as the 'centre of pressure'. The relationship between the positions of the centre of gravity and the centre of pressure is a vital part of aircraft design.

A glider with part of its wing removed to show the aerofoil section.

(Courtesy Bernard Baldwin)

ANGLE OF ATTACK

Whenever a wing section passes through the air at a different angle relative to the airflow its lifting qualities are changed. The angle it makes with the airflow is known as the 'angle of attack'. It is a fact that as the angle of attack increases, the lift increases in direct proportion. However, this is true only up to a certain critical value. At this critical value the lift disappears almost completely and the plane stalls.

Pilots make use of the extra lift created by increasing the angle of attack within the safety limit in order to land smoothly. Reducing speed to land decreases the lift from the wings and there is a danger of dropping too rapidly. However, just as the plane is about to touch down the pilot raises the nose slightly. This increases the angle of attack and the extra lift slows the rate of descent. The plane then drops smoothly and gently on to the runway.

10

MOTION IN THREE DIMENSIONS

We have already stated that the motion of an aeroplane can be separated into the motion of the centre of gravity and motion about the centre of gravity.

In aviation it is usual to separate the rotations about the centre of gravity into three components called pitch, roll and yaw. The axes of these rotations are at right angles to one another.

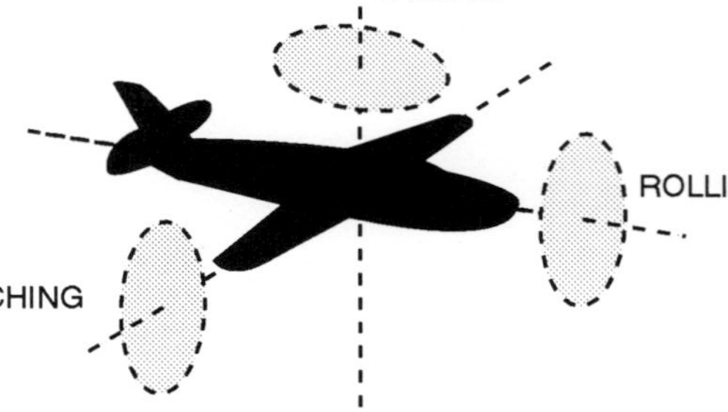

PITCHING

YAWING

ROLLING

Any change from straight and level flight is considered as motion about one of these three axes.

CONTROLLING PITCH

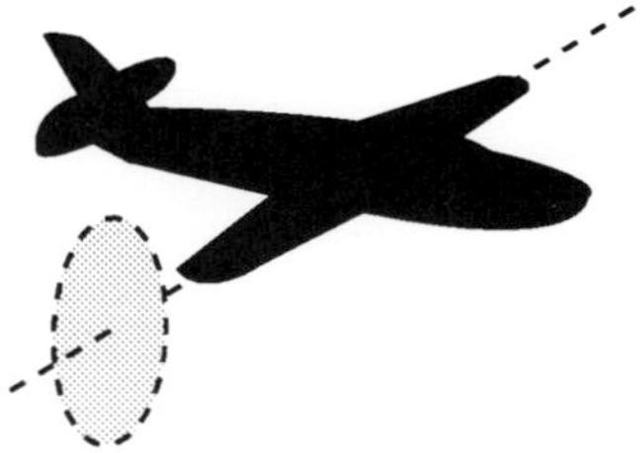

A change of pitch causes the nose to go up or down. Since this alters both the angle of attack and the position of the centre of lift, it is important that there is some automatic restoring force to prevent a sudden dive or climb. An integral part of the design of any plane is to arrange that the forces of lift, gravity and those from the airflows over the tailplane correct any pitching automatically. Planes without a tailplane, such as deltawings, are more unstable and difficult to control. The tips of the wings have to be set as far back as possible in order to compensate for the missing tailplane.

CONTROLLING ROLL

When a plane rolls, one wing becomes lower than the other and the plane begins to slip downwards and sideways. Such a motion is known as 'sideslip' and is obviously very dangerous if it is allowed to continue. On Page 11 we saw how a plane with dihedral automatically develops a restoring force to bring the plane back to level. You will see this in operation on both model planes. Look out for a slight wobble either side of level as they correct themselves in flight. In full size planes the main control for roll is a set of moveable flaps along the rear edges of the wings, called ailerons.

15

MINIBOOK SECTION F

STABLE FLIGHT - AVOIDING TURNING MOMENTS

The motion of any aeroplane can be regarded as the combination of two types of motion;

'The motion *of* the centre of gravity'
'The motion *about* the centre of gravity'.

If the lift is equal to the weight, then there can be no vertical acceleration. However, the plane itself could still begin to rotate about the centre of gravity if the turning moments are not zero.

Turning moment = force × perpendicular distance to the force

anticlockwise turning moment

If the lift acts behind the centre of gravity there is a turning moment which causes the nose to pitch downwards and the plane to dive.

clockwise turning moment

If the lift acts forward of the centre of gravity there is a turning moment, which causes the nose to pitch upwards and the plane to climb or possibly stall from the increased angle of attack.

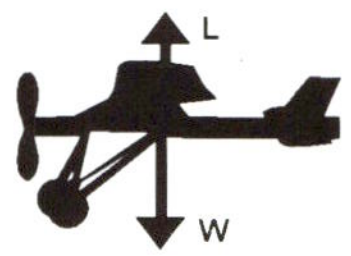

Only if the centre of gravity and centre of pressure are in the same vertical line will the plane fly straight and level. In these circumstances the perpendicular distance from the centre of gravity to the lift force is zero and so the turning moment is also zero. This stable situation can be reached in the models by adding paper clips or Blu-Tack to them. By adding extra weight in this way, the CG can be moved to the same vertical line as the centre of pressure.

WINGS WITH DIHEDRAL

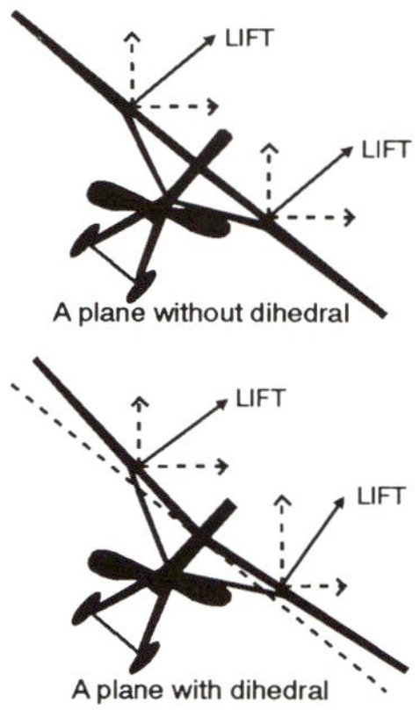

You will have noticed that the wings of both models slope up a little. This is known as 'dihedral'. It is an important design feature which greatly increases the stability of an aeroplane.

When the wings tilt, the force of lift remains at right angles to the new wing position. The vertical component of the lift is now insufficient to balance the weight and so the plane begins to accelerate downwards. At the same time the lift has a horizontal component and so the plane slips sideways. This combination of motions is called 'sideslip' and needs urgent action on the part of the pilot if it is not to prove fatal.

A plane without dihedral

A plane with dihedral

With dihedral the position is much more stable. The plane still begins to sideslip but now the lower or inner wing presents a greater angle of attack than the other, generating more lift and rolling it back to the level. In planes without a pilot a certain amount of dihedral is essential.

Certain military planes are constructed to have negative dihedral. This makes them unstable but highly maneuvrable. The instability is then too great even for an active pilot to manage and such planes need to be under continuous computer control.

11

HOW DOES AN AEROPLANE TAKE OFF?

Now that we have an understanding of the four forces of lift, weight, thrust and drag which act on an aeroplane, we can explain how it takes off as it accelerates along the runway.

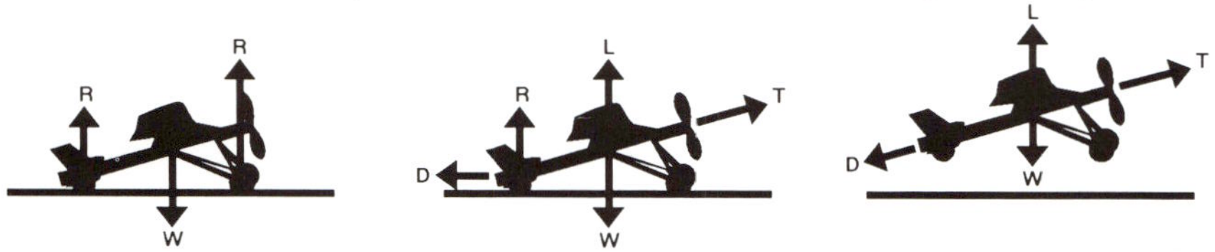

While the plane is waiting to take off on a still day there is no lift because no air is passing over the wings. All the weight is supported by the reaction of the wheels on the ground. As the propeller begins to turn and the thrust becomes greater than the drag, it begins to move forwards. Air passes over the wings, generating some lift and reducing the reaction from the ground. As the speed increases there comes a time when the lift becomes great enough to exceed the weight. No further reaction is then needed from the ground and the plane lifts off.

HOW HIGH CAN A PLANE FLY?

At higher altitudes the air is thinner and there is a smaller pressure difference between the upper and lower surfaces of the wings. They therefore provide less lift. However, at the same time the thinner air means that the drag is reduced and an engine of a given size can drive the plane faster. This extra speed increases the lift and compensates to some extent for the reduction due to the air being thinner. Another factor to consider is that at higher altitudes there is less oxygen for the engine to burn and this reduces the thrust it can produce. At a certain height and speed the maximum thrust equals the drag and the lift equals the weight. When all the forces and influences balance, the plane can go no higher.

THE BEST HEIGHT TO FLY

For passenger planes, the higher the better. Most airliners fly at between 30,000 and 40,000 ft. (9 to 12km), just within the stratosphere. At that height the air is smoother as it is less affected by the weather systems below. There is also no chance of crashing into a mountain! At such altitudes the air pressure and the oxygen content are both too low for human survival and so the air pressure in the cabin has to be maintained artificially. Keeping it as it is at sea level would place too much of a strain on the structure and so it is maintained at a pressure similar to natural air found at 8,000 ft.

For military planes, the situation is quite different. At one time it was possible for bombers or spy planes to fly so high that they could not be attacked by enemy fighter planes. However, they can now be detected by radar and brought down by missiles. Nowadays, to confuse the radar, modern military planes have to fly as close to the ground as possible and need to have excellent navigation systems and to be highly maneuvrable.

EXOSPHERE
500 Km
IONOSPHERE
85 Km
MESOSPHERE
50 Km
STRATOSPHERE
10 Km
TROPOSPHERE
EVEREST
EARTH

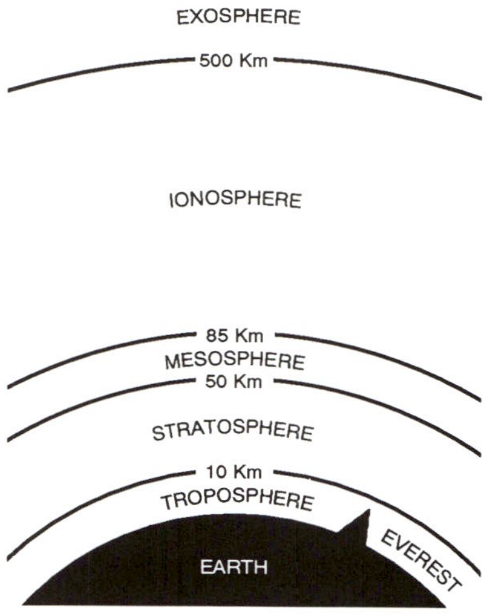

THE FIVE LAYERS OF THE ATMOSPHERE

14

THRUST - PROPELLING THE PLANE FORWARDS

The forces of lift and weight determine the vertical motion of the plane. To deal with its horizontal motion we now have to deal with the horizontal forces of thrust and drag.

Thrust is the name of the force which propels the plane in the direction we wish it to go. It can be provided by a propeller or by a jet engine. Certain high altitude planes can also be propelled by rocket engines or boosters.

The quantity 'mass x velocity' is known as momentum. Forces therefore cause changes in momentum. In order to appreciate how engines of any kind develop thrust, we need to use the idea of momentum. A good way to understand how both propellers or jet engines work is to start with a cannon and a cannon ball with the barrel pointing horizontally.

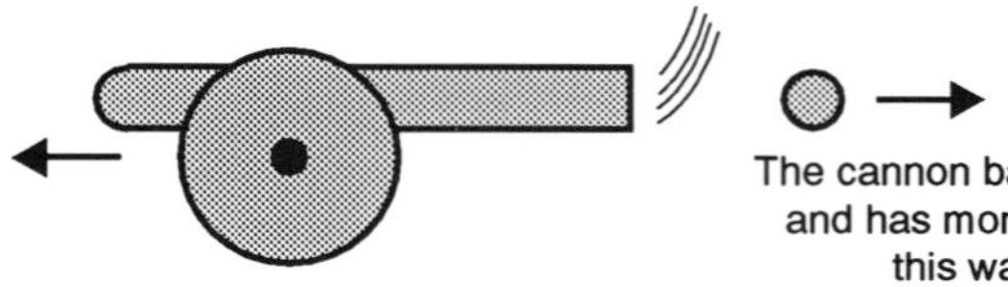

Force = mass x acceleration = mass x rate of change of velocity
= rate of change of (mass x velocity)

The cannon recoils and has momentum this way

The cannon ball is fired and has momentum this way

Before it fires, both the cannon and the cannon ball are stationary and so they each have no momentum. When the gunpowder explodes, the expanding gases exert a force on both the gun and the cannon ball. These forces are equal and opposite. Since the forces are equal they cause equal changes in momentum but in opposite directions.

momentum of cannon = momentum of cannon ball
mass of cannon x velocity of cannon = mass of cannon ball x velocity of cannon ball

The cannon ball is propelled towards its target and the cannon recoils. Although they each have the same amount of momentum they do not move with the same velocity. The cannon has much more mass than the ball and therefore recoils less rapidly.

Essentially aeroplanes are propelled by giving momentum to air molecules.

THRUST FROM A JET ENGINE

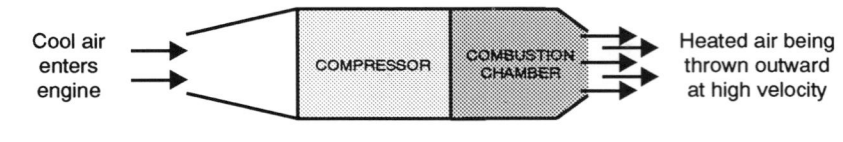

Cool air enters engine

COMPRESSOR

COMBUSTION CHAMBER

Heated air being thrown outward at high velocity

A jet engine works by firing out molecules at very high speed. Each one is like a very small cannon ball and imparts a small amount of momentum in the opposite direction to the engine. The engine is firmly attached to the plane and thrusts it forward. By throwing out tonnes and tonnes of air and gases every second, a jet engine can provide thrust for a very large plane.

A rocket motor works in the same way, but the gases which are thrown out are generated by burning fuel which contains its own oxygen. Having no need of air, such engines can travel out to space. Jet engines are only efficient up to a certain height - a maximum of about 70,000 ft (21km.).

12

THRUST FROM A PROPELLER

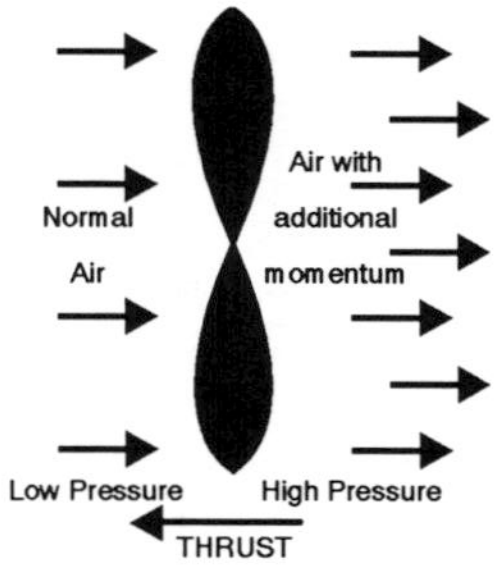

A propeller is really a rotating wing and it has an aerofoil shape. The engine moves the propeller and so imparts energy and momentum to air molecules in the direction opposite to that in which the plane wishes to travel. In other words, there is low air pressure in front of the propeller and a high pressure behind. The change of momentum which is given to the air molecules is balanced exactly by an equal and opposite change of momentum given to the propeller. The propeller is attached to the plane which therefore flies forwards. It does not matter whether the propeller is at the front or the back of the plane. The path of a propeller tip through the air gives the propeller its alternative name - the airscrew.

THRUST

Low Pressure ← Normal Air → Air with additional momentum → High Pressure

DRAG - RESISTANCE TO MOTION

Whenever anything moves through the air it has to push molecules aside. The force taken to do this is called air resistance. In aeronautical situations the sum of all kinds of air resistance is called 'drag'. It is force which acts in opposition to 'thrust'.

One might think that air molecules just ahead of an aeroplane or ones which have passed over the wings or propeller would have no influence on the motion of the plane. This is not the case. Remember that individual molecules are moving randomly at an average speed of 450 m/sec (1000 m.p.h.), much faster than any but supersonic planes. The influence of a plane spreads all around it and the energy required to exert the influence is part of the drag. A simple proof of the existence of influence ahead of a plane is that you can hear a subsonic plane coming towards you.

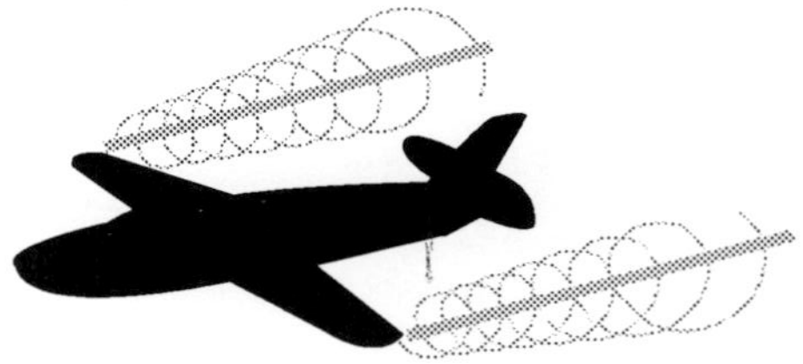

An important characteristic of the flow of air over a wing is the creation of vortices - swirling masses of air by the wing tips. A good proportion of the drag of an aeroplane is created by these vortices and in certain weather conditions they can be seen as wispy spiral trails.

Much thought has been given to reducing the drag due to these vortices by modifying the design of the wings. It was noticed that soaring birds such as vultures and condors have special feathers at the end of their wings which help to reduce them. Various attempts have been made to find mechanical equivalents, but they have not generally been adopted.

Aeroplanes have to be designed so that the resultant force of thrust and the resultant force of drag act in the same line through the centre of gravity. Otherwise there would be a turning moment whenever the forces were not equal and the plane would become unstable and difficult to control.

13

GENERAL INSTRUCTIONS

Make one model at a time and it is probably best to make the Helicopter first, then the Monoplane and to leave the Deltawing till last. All the paper and card for the models is included in the book but you also need some extra items. These extra items are listed inside the front cover. Each model is constructed from two or more units and it is best to complete one before starting another.

SCORING

Scoring is very important if you want to make accurate models. It makes the paper or card fold cleanly and accurately along the line you want. Use a ball point pen which has run out of ink and rule firmly along the fold lines. Experienced model makers may use a craft knife but it needs care not to cut right through the paper.

● ● MAKING THE HOLES ● ●

Holes are needed for the press-studs, matchsticks and the wire axle. They are marked on the models with the symbols above. Use the point of a pair of dividers or compasses to get each hole started. You can then enlarge it by twisting the tool round and round. Another way is to push the point of a ball point pen into the initial hole and to gently rotate it until the hole becomes just big enough. Be careful not to overdo it.

CUTTING AND FOLDING

1. Cut out all the pieces for your chosen unit keeping well away from the outline.
2. Score along all score lines, dotted and solid. The score lines are all printed in black ink.
3. Cut out precisely.

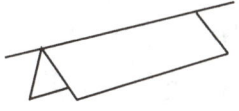

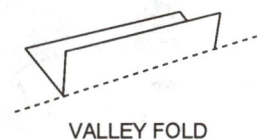

HILL FOLD   VALLEY FOLD

4. Fold away from you along solid lines to make hill folds and towards you along dotted lines to make valley folds. Crease firmly.

THE HELICOPTER

A. MAKING THE FUSELAGE
Follow the general instructions above to cut, score and fold the three pieces of this unit which are on pages 1 & 35. Then glue them together in numerical order.

B. MAKING THE POWER UNIT
The instructions are inside the back cover.

C. THREADING THE ELASTIC
Pierce the two holes in the fuselage, using the method described above. Then tie a piece of fine string to the loop of model elastic at the knot. Hold the fuselage upright and allow the other end of the string to drop downwards through it. Then pull the string and ease the cap into place.
Pull the string a little harder in order to stretch it. You can then insert the matchstick within the loop of the elastic.
Your Helicopter is now ready to fly.

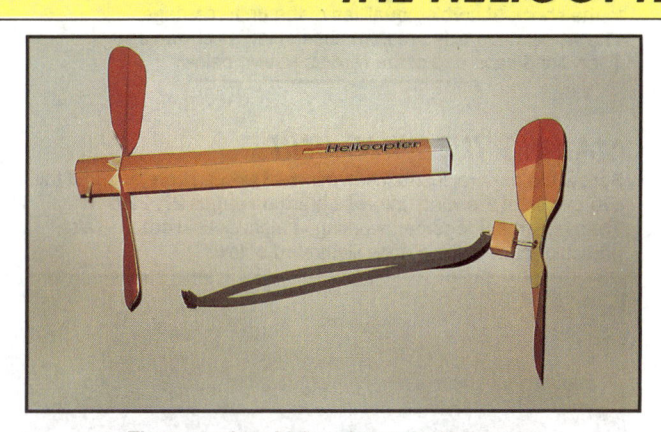

The two units which make up the Helicopter
There are hints and suggestions about this model and how to trim it to fly well on page 21 of the minibook.

THE DELTAWING

A. MAKING THE FUSELAGE
Follow the general instructions above to cut, score and fold the five pieces of the fuselage which are on pages 3 & 5. Then glue them together in alphabetical order.

B. MAKING THE WING UNIT
Cut, score and fold the seven pieces of the wing unit, which are on pages 5, 7, 9 & 11, again following the general instructions above. Then glue them together in alphabetical order. Pay careful attention to the assembly of the wings in order to establish the dihedral correctly. It is very important to spread glue along the top edge of the wing spars. Complete the model by glueing the wing unit to the fuselage, making sure to check that it faces forwards and that it is placed symmetrically. Look carefully from both the top and the front before the glue sets.

D. MAKING THE POWER UNIT
The instructions are inside the back cover.

E. THREADING THE ELASTIC
Pierce the two holes in the fuselage, using the method described above. Then tie a piece of fine string to the loop of model elastic at the knot. Hold the fuselage upright and allow the other end of the string to drop downwards through it. Then pull the string and ease the cap into place.
Pull the string a little harder in order to stretch it. You can then insert the matchstick within the loop of the elastic.
Your Deltawing is now ready to fly.

The three units which make up the Deltawing
There are hints and instructions about this model and how to trim it to fly well on page 23 of the minibook.

THE MONOPLANE

A. MAKING THE FUSELAGE

Follow the general instructions overleaf to cut, score and fold the thirteen pieces of this unit, which are on pages 33 & 35. Then glue the fuselage together, working in numerical order.
Pierce the holes at the centre of each wheel and at the end of the struts using the method described overleaf. Then mount a press-stud on each wheel to act as a hub.

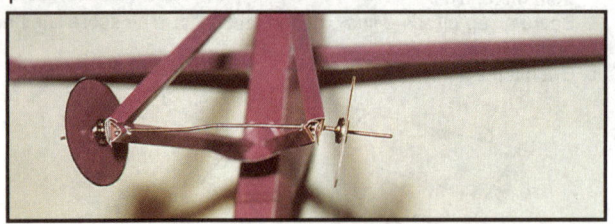

Straighten a paper clip to make the wire axle. This axle passes through the holes near the end of the struts and freely through the holes at the centre of each press-stud. Use a drawing pin to enlarge the hole if necessary. You want the smallest hole possible which allows the wire to turn freely.
Do not glue the ends of the struts together as their flexibility adds to the shock-absorbing qualities of the undercarriage.
The wheels and axle are then assembled as shown above.
Then bend each end of the wire as shown below.

The four units which make up the Monoplane
There are hints and instructions about this model and how to trim it to fly well on page 22 of the minibook.

B. MAKING THE WING UNIT

Follow the general instructions overleaf to cut, score and fold the five pieces of the wing unit, which are on pages 27, 29 & 31. Then glue them together, working in alphabetical order. Take particular care at the stages illustrated below.

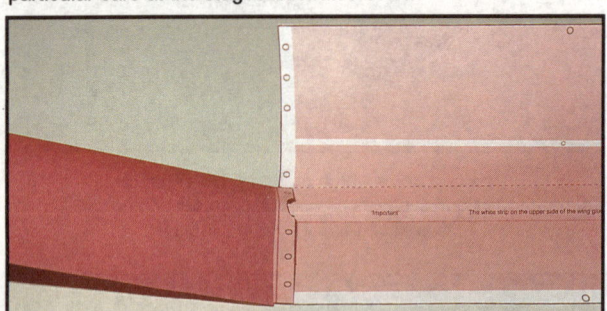

It is most important that glue is spread along the top edge of the wing spars before the top surface of the wing is pulled over and glued into place. If this glue is missed, the lifting qualities of the wing are very much reduced.

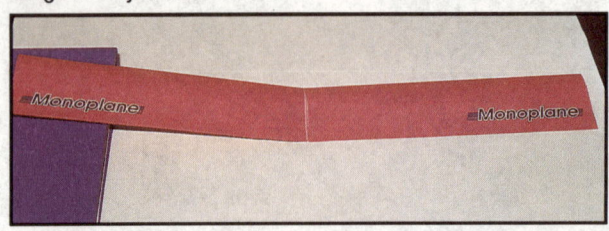

Prop up the left wing with a book before completing the right wing. It is the glueing of flaps N and O into their correct positions which creates the dihedral.
As you glue the wing unit to the fuselage and the spars, be sure to check that it faces forwards and is placed symmetrically. Look carefully from the top and the front before the glue sets.

C. MAKING THE TAIL UNIT

Follow the general instructions overleaf to cut, score and fold the five pieces of this unit, which are on page 31. Then glue the pieces together, working in alphabetical order. When it is complete it is not glued to the fuselage but slides over it.

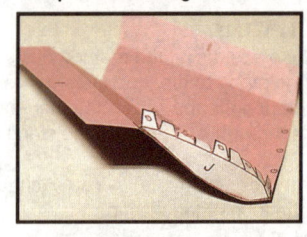

These photographs show two stages in making the tail unit.

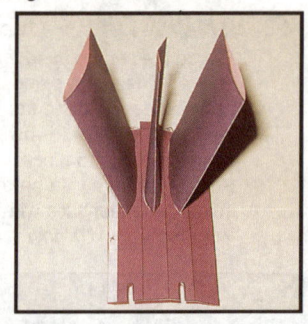

D. MAKING THE POWER UNIT

The instructions are inside the back cover.

E. THREADING THE ELASTIC

Pierce the two holes in the fuselage, using the method described overleaf. Then tie a piece of fine string to the loop of model elastic at the knot. Hold the fuselage upright and allow the other end of the string to drop downwards through it. Then pull the string and ease the cap into place.
Pull the string a little harder in order to stretch it. You can then insert the matchstick within the loop of the elastic. Finally slide the tail unit into position.
Your Monoplane is now ready to fly.

MAKING THE MINIBOOK

1. Remove the six pages which make the minibook.
2. Score along the lines marked ▶◀ 
3. Cut out precisely.
4. Fold away from you to make a hill fold.
5. Assemble the sections to make the 24 page minibook.
6. Fix them together. If you have a suitable stapler then that is probably the easiest way. Otherwise use a needle and thread like the bookbinders of old!

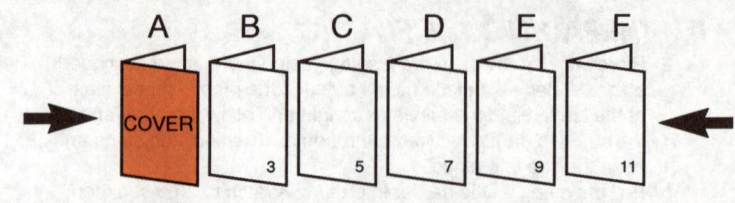

Do a careful check that the pages are in the correct order.

Monoplane

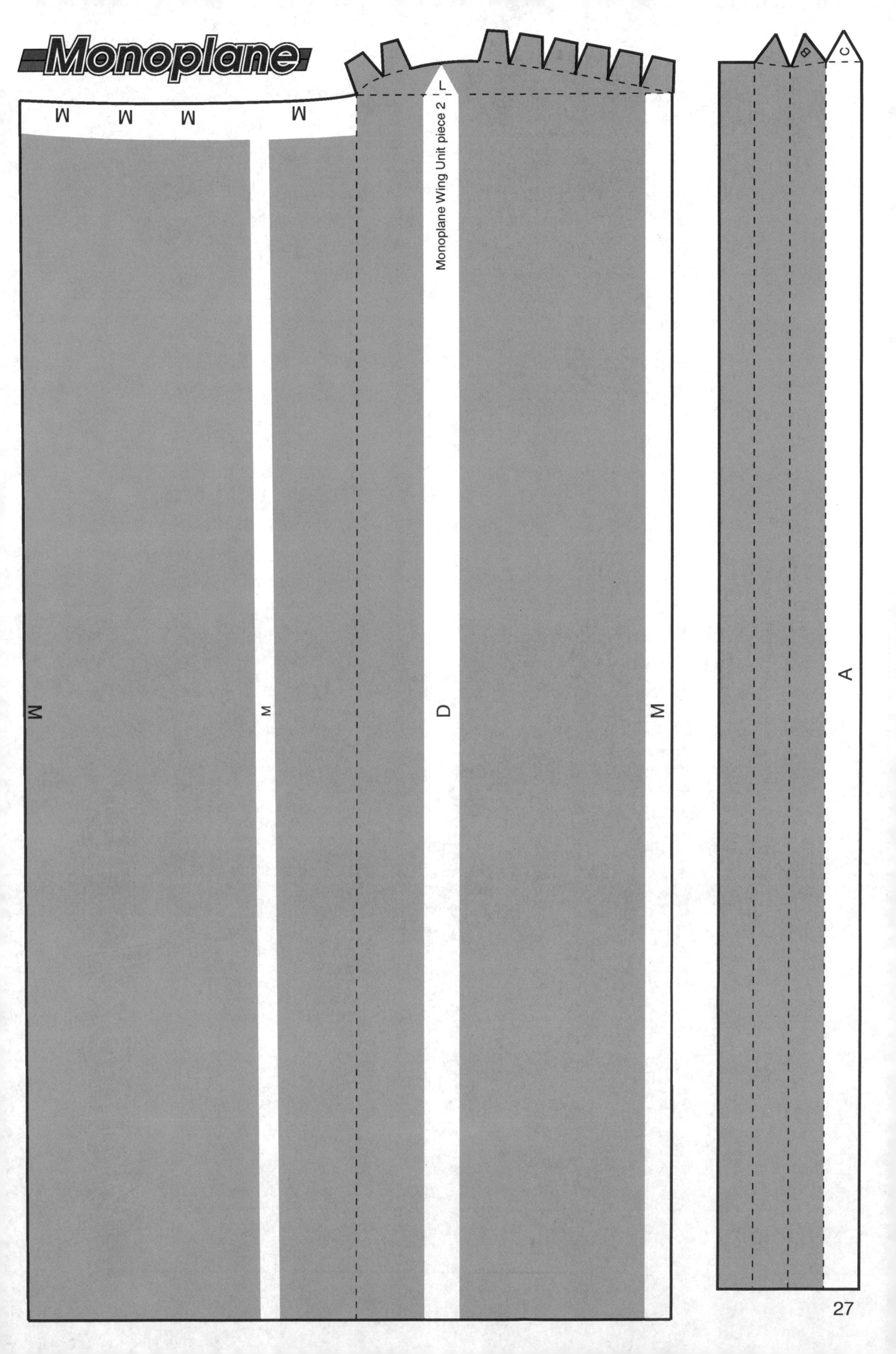

Monoplane Wing Unit piece 2

Monoplane Wing Unit piece 1

'Important'

The white strip on the upper side of the wing glues to the top of this spar.

'Important'

Monoplane

Monoplane

Monoplane Wiing Unit piece 4

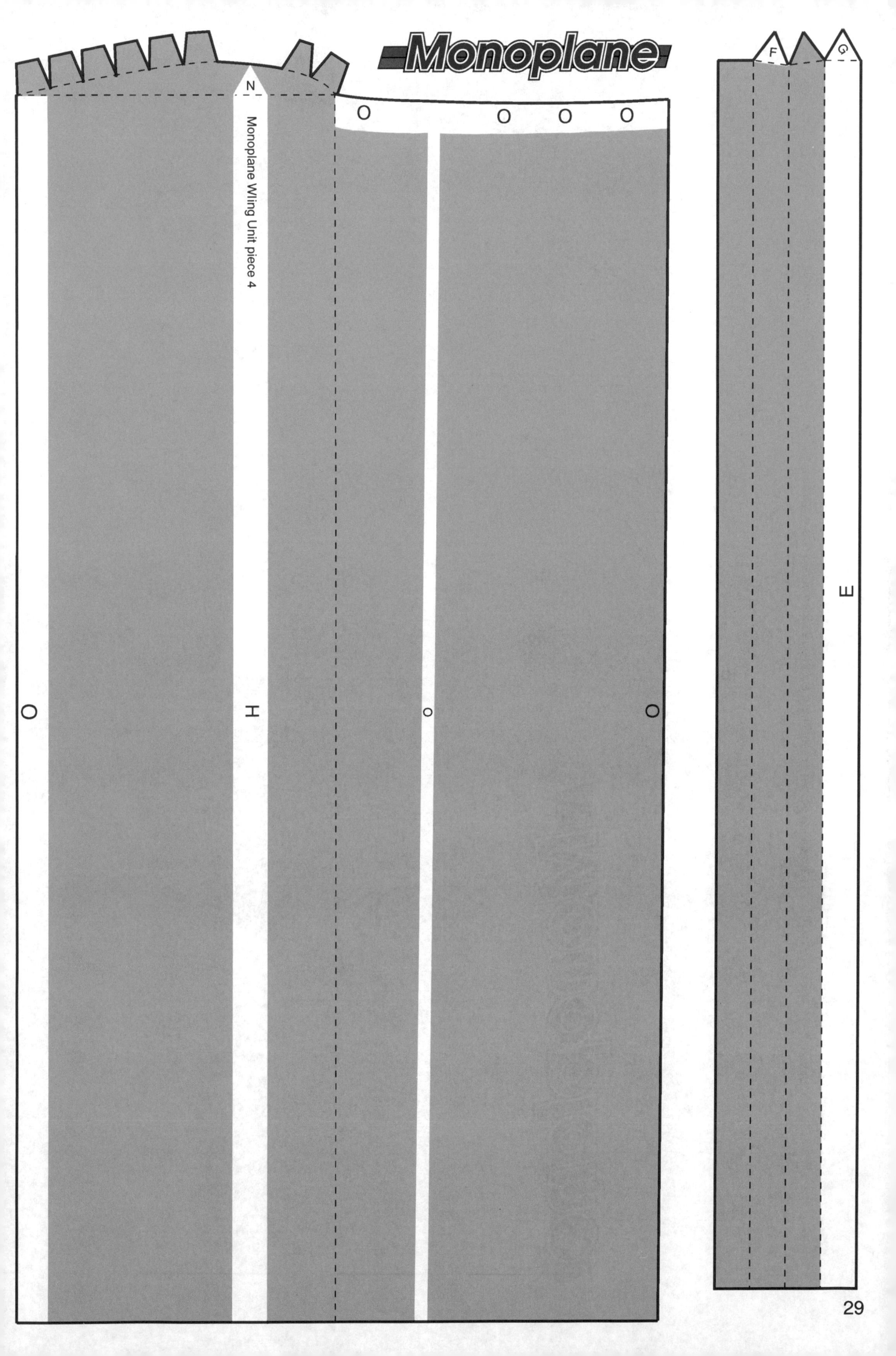

G

F

N Monoplane Wing Unit piece 3

'important'

The white strip on the upper side of the wing glues to the top of this spar.

E

H

'important'

Monoplane

30

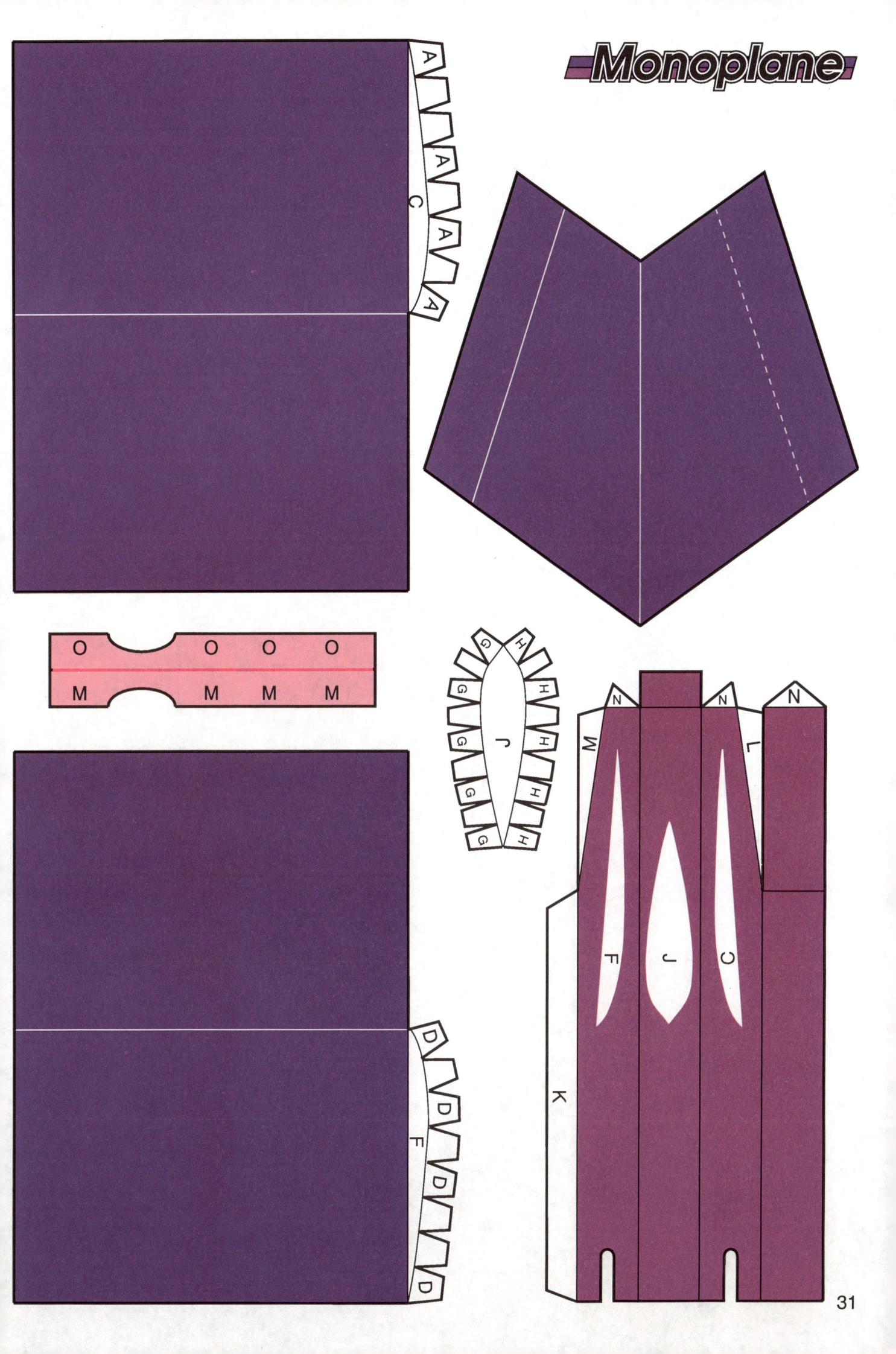

Monoplane

31

Monoplane Tail Unit piece 1
Monoplane Tail Unit piece 4
Monoplane Tail Unit piece 3
Monoplane Tail Unit piece 5
Monoplane Tail Unit piece 2
Monoplane Wing Unit piece 5

Monoplane

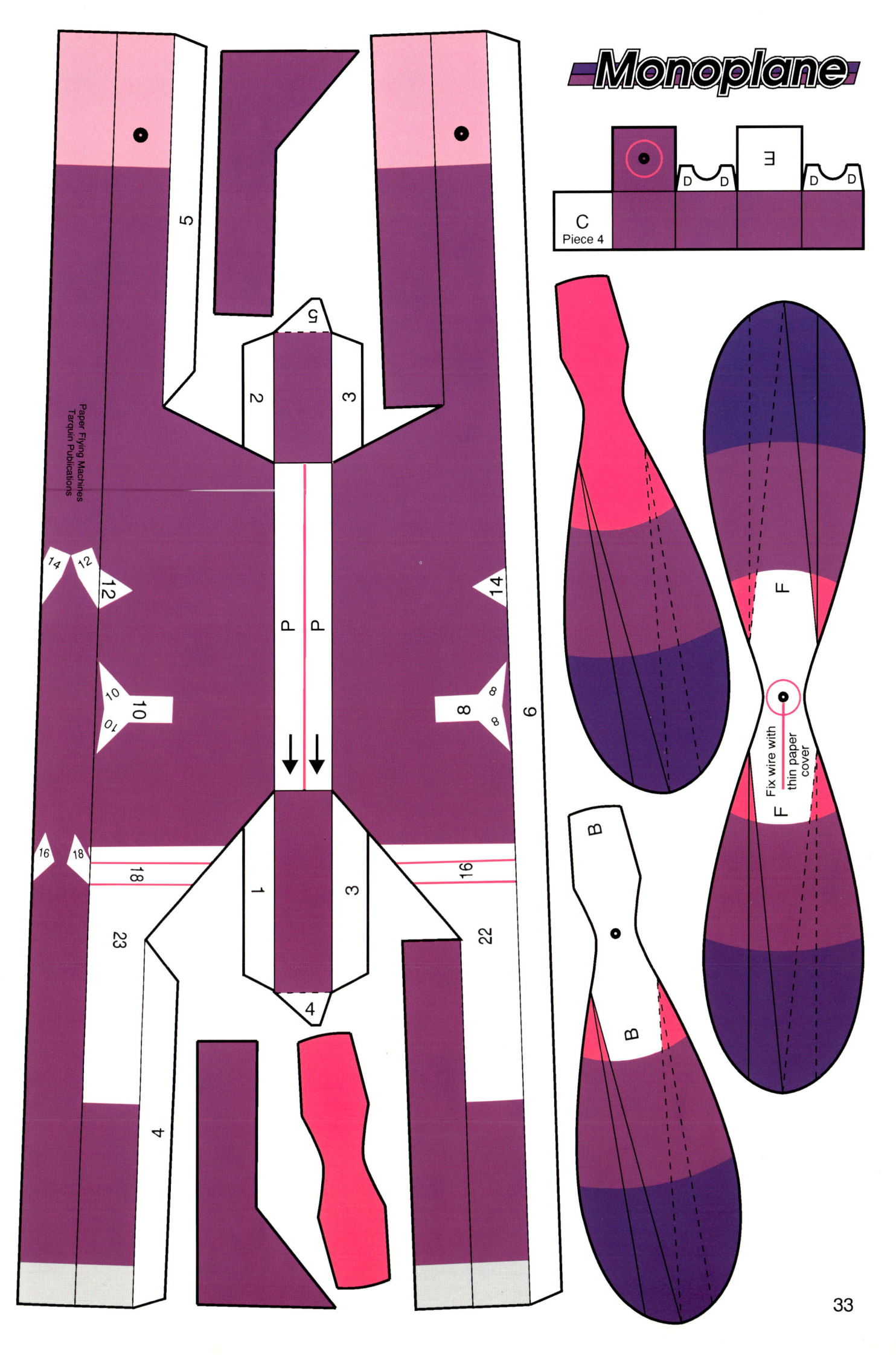

C Piece 4

Paper Flying Machines
Tarquin Publications

Fix wire with thin paper cover

33

34

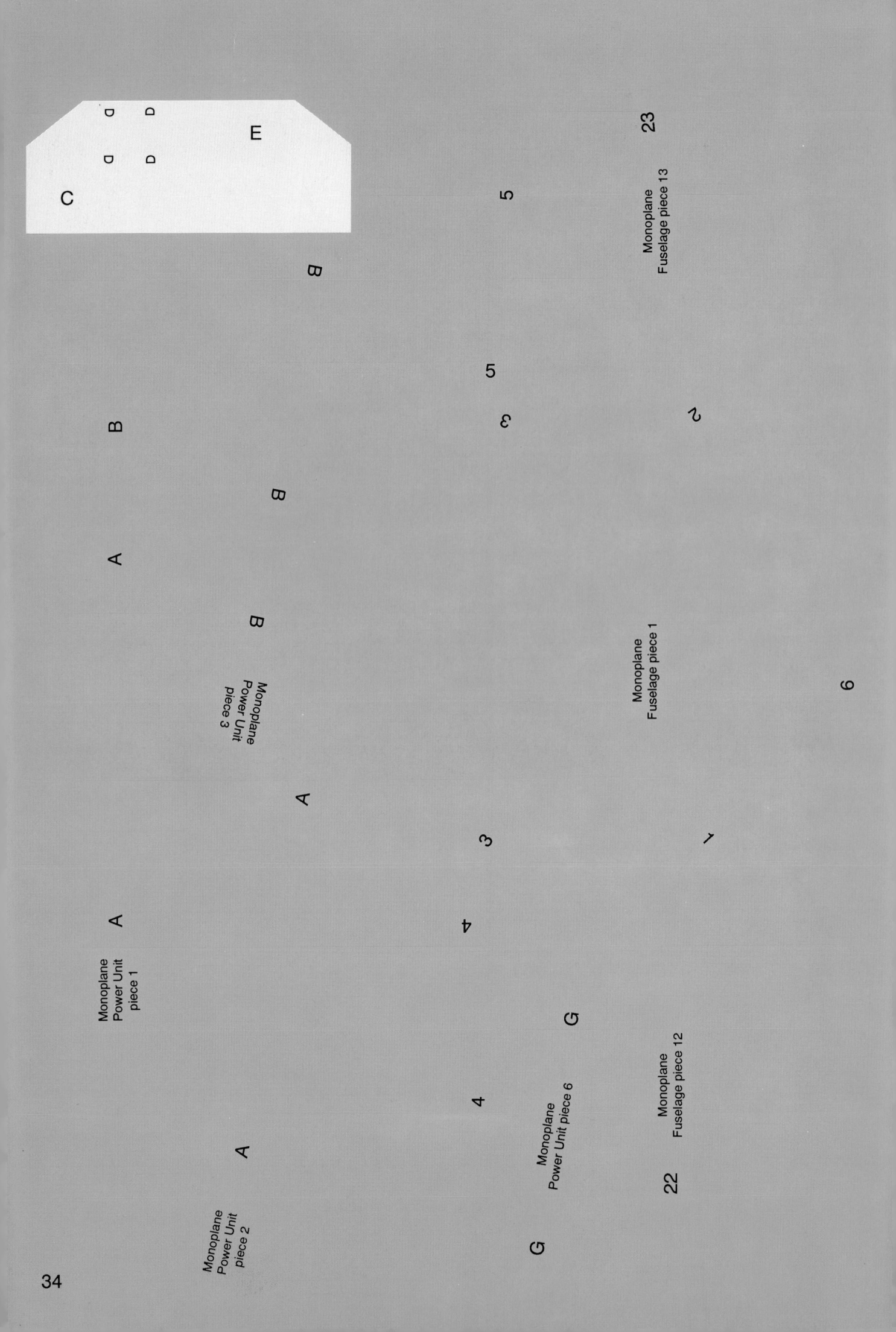

Helicopter

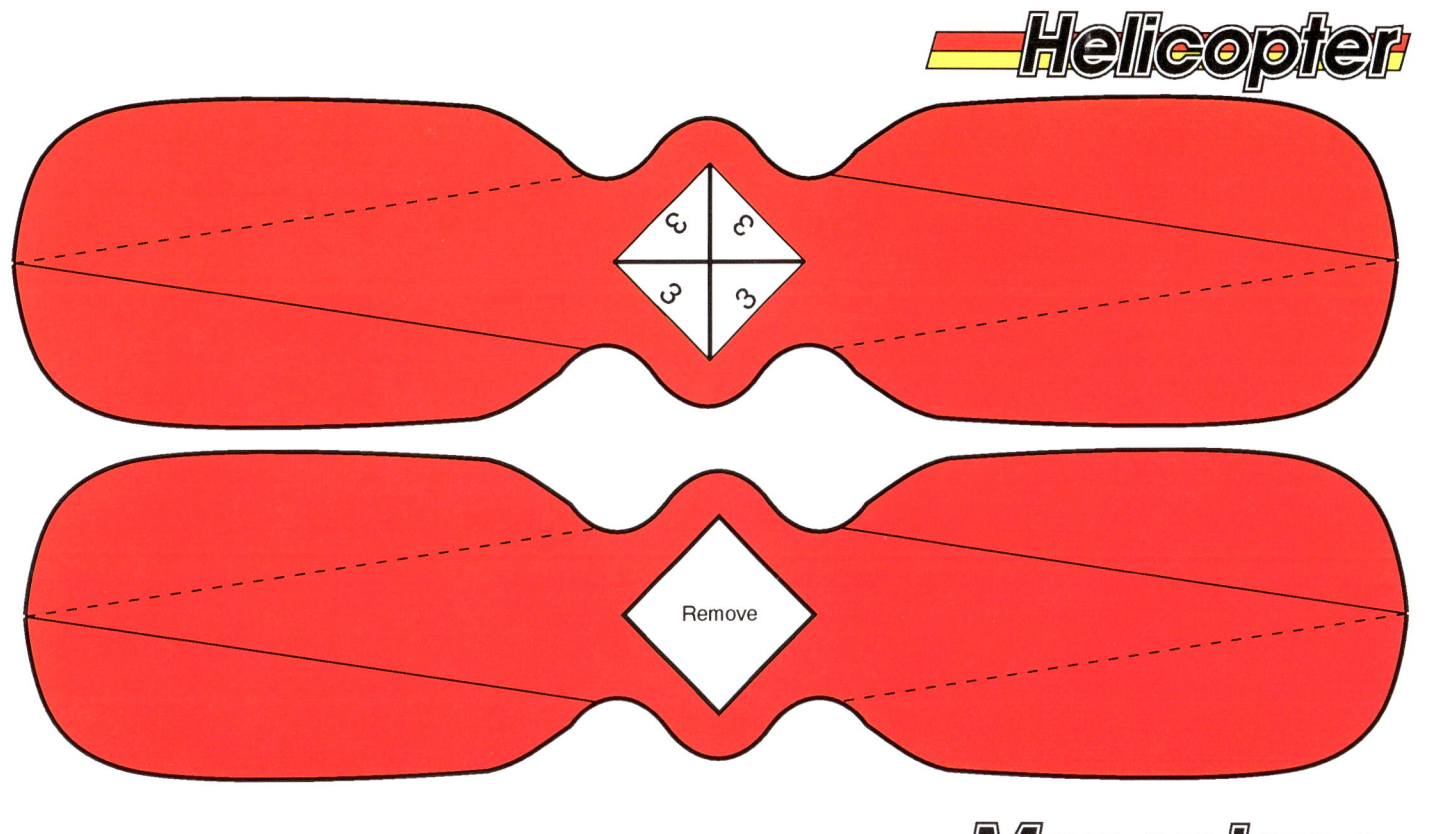

Monoplane

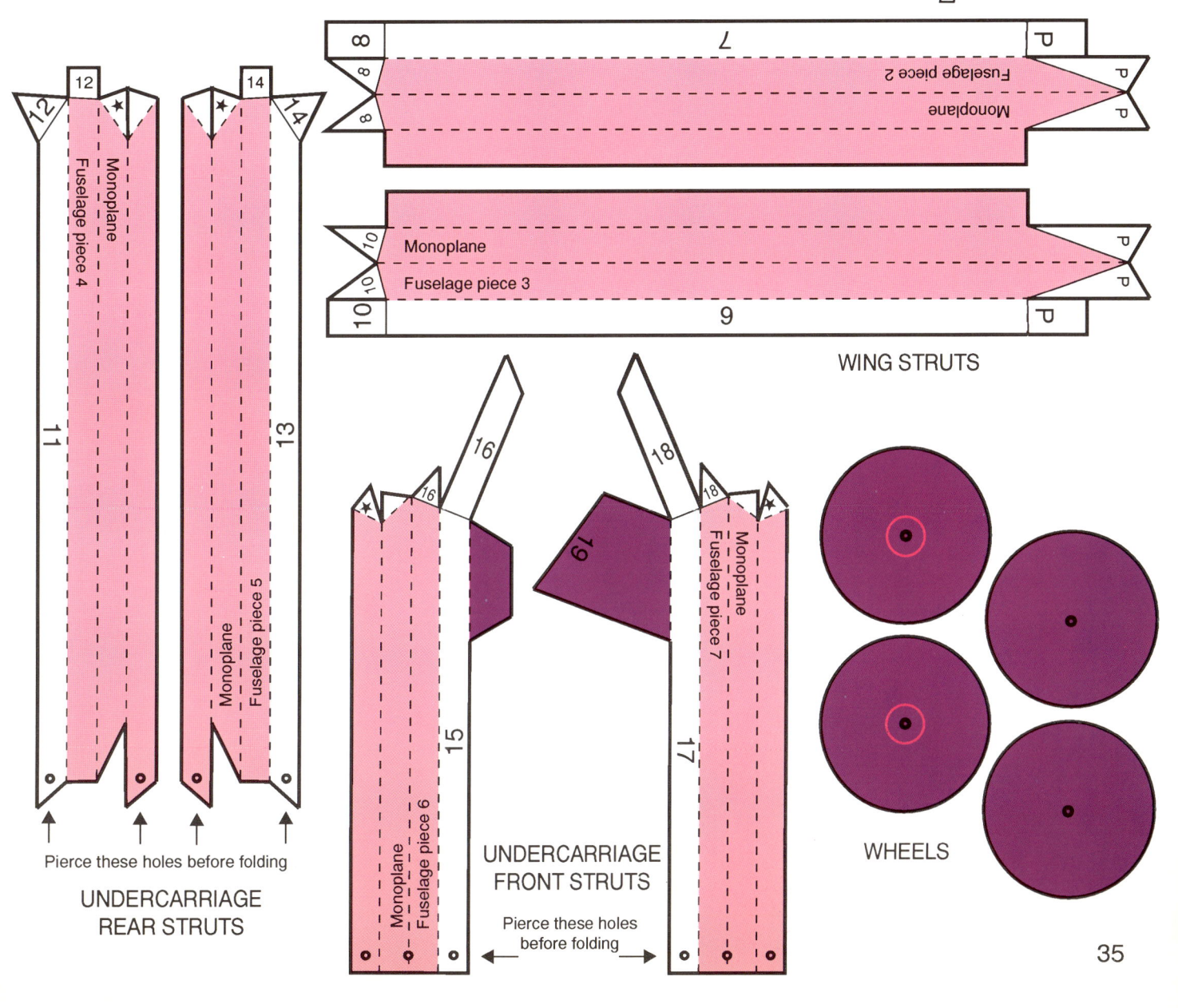

WING STRUTS

UNDERCARRIAGE REAR STRUTS

Pierce these holes before folding

UNDERCARRIAGE FRONT STRUTS

Pierce these holes before folding

WHEELS

35

Helicopter
Fuselage piece 2   2

2

Helicopter
Fuselage piece 3   2

2

7
6

13 11

20
Monoplane
Fuselage
piece 8

20
Monoplane
Fuselage
piece 9

21
Monoplane
Fuselage
piece 10

19

21
Monoplane
Fuselage
piece 11

17

15

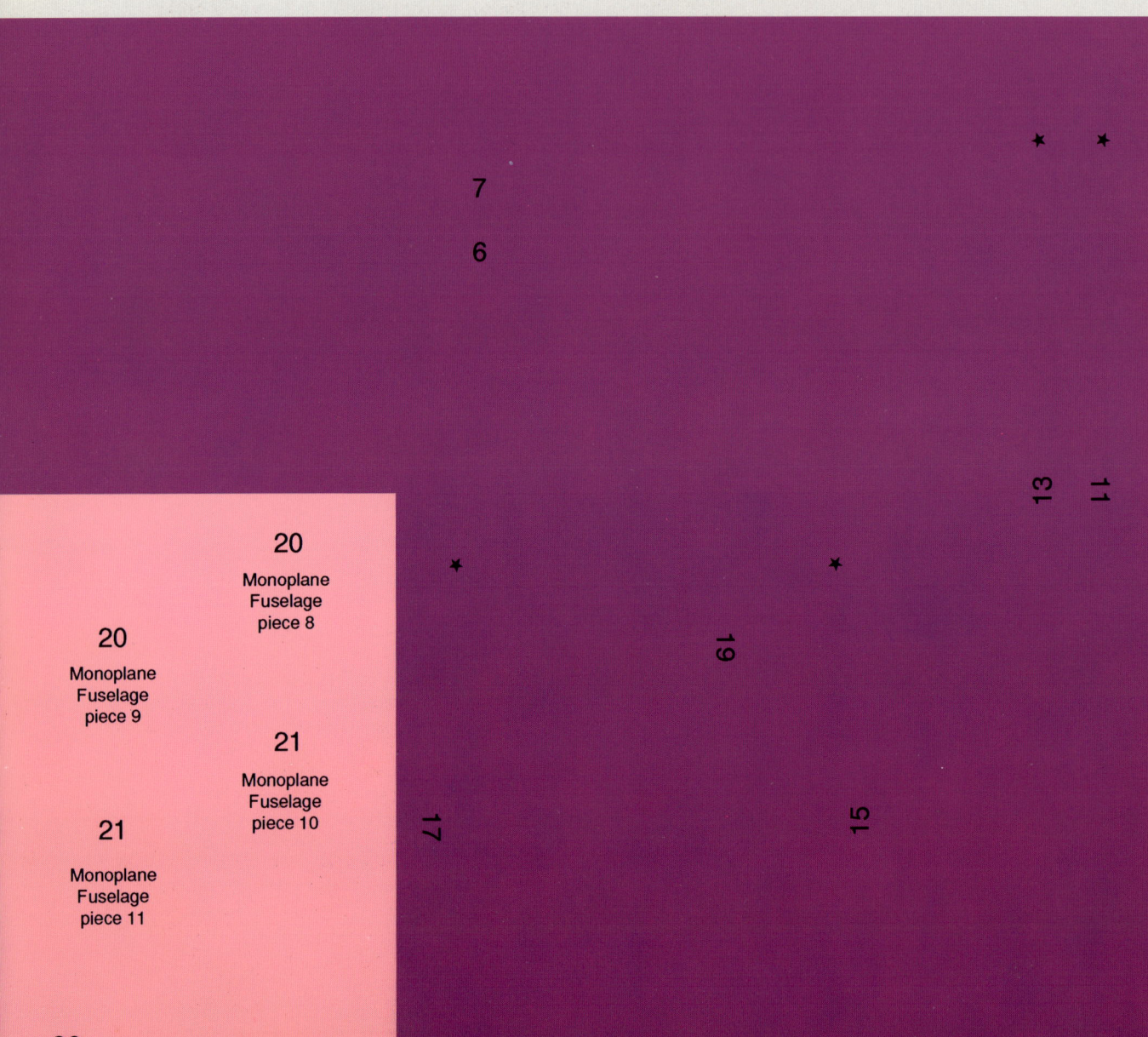

36